P9-DNU-019

CROCHETED Afghans

Oxmoor House®

© 1988 by Oxmoor House, Inc.
Book Division of Southern Progress Corporation
P.O. Box 2463, Birmingham, Alabama 35201

All rights reserved. No part of this book may be
reproduced in any form or by any means without
the prior written permission of the publisher, ex-
cepting brief quotations in connection with reviews
written specifically for inclusion in magazines or
newspapers.

Library of Congress Catalog Number: 87-62732
ISBN: 0-8487-0738-9
Manufactured in the United States of America
First Printing 1988

Executive Editor: Candace N. Conard
Production Manager: Jerry Higdon
Associate Production Manager: Rick Litton
Art Director: Bob Nance

Crocheted Afghans

Editor: Carol Cook Hagood
Assistant Editor: Margaret Allen Northen
Copy Chief: Mary Jean Haddin
Production Assistant: Theresa L. Beste
Designer: Diana Smith Morrison
Artists: Barbara Ball, Larry Hunter

Contents

Introduction

Amanda loves rainbows. They dance on the walls of her room, glimmer in ribbon-trimmed pillows, and gleam in dresser-top keepsakes. When I saw the Over the Rainbow afghan (page 47), I knew it was perfect for my red-haired five-year-old—a more "grown-up" version of the toddler blanket she had so dearly loved and (it seemed to me) so quickly outgrown.

We were lucky; the yarn was available in rich pastels to match her wallpaper. A smaller hook produced plump, soft stitches, less open than those of the original (and less likely to catch little toes). For a child-size piece, I used only seven stripes and reduced the width to twenty-eight inches. I added a soft, multicolored fringe tied with picot ribbon (for the girl who loves the shine of satin), and funny buttons (yellow ducks, rosy gingerbread men, pink bunnies) to make her smile as daydreams drift into dreams. It's the same afghan, but with little changes that make it Amanda's own.

As you turn through this first-ever collection of afghans from Oxmoor House, we think you'll find many designs you'll be eager to share. Make them just as you see them here, or choose colors to suit your surroundings and please those closest to your heart. We've had genuine fun in bringing these beautiful designs to you—and now the fun is yours. So, go ahead—make your own rainbows!

Carol Cook Hagood
Editor

Spring

Dancing Ducks

Daffodil-bright and downy soft, these springtime ducks will dance into your heart. Stitch them in squares of filet crochet wound with a ribbon bow.

FINISHED SIZE
Approximately 36" x 44".

MATERIALS
Yarn description: Sportweight acrylic.
Yarn pictured: Coats & Clark Red Heart® Luster Sheen®, Art. A.94, 2-oz. skeins, 12 Pale Yellow.
Other: White satin ribbon (⅝" wide), 7 yd.

TOOLS AND EQUIPMENT
Size D crochet hook, or size to obtain gauge; tapestry needle.

GAUGE
Filet block: 3 mesh = 1"
Solid block: 6 rows = 1"

DIRECTIONS
Filet block (make 5): Ch 69.

Row 1: Dc in 6th ch from hook, * ch 1, sk 1 ch, dc in next ch, rep from * across = 32 mesh. Ch 4, turn (Row 1 of chart completed).

Row 2: Dc in next dc, * ch 1, dc in next dc, rep from * across, end by sk 2 chs on starting ch, dc in next ch. Ch 4, turn (Row 2 of chart completed).

Row 3: Following Row 3 of chart [dc in next dc, ch 1] 10 times, dc in next dc, dc in ch-1 sp (filled mesh over open mesh completed), [dc in next dc, ch 1] twice, dc in next dc, dc in ch-1 sp, [dc in next dc, ch 1] twice, [dc in next dc, dc in ch-1 sp] twice, * dc in next dc, ch 1; rep from * across, end with dc in 3rd ch of turning ch.

Rows 4–38: Continue following chart as established. At the end of Row 38, fasten off.

Solid block (make 4): Ch 66.

Row 1: Sk 2 ch, * sc in next ch, ch 1, sk 1 ch; rep from * across, end with sc in last ch = 32 ch-1 lps. Ch 1, turn.

Row 2: Sc in first sc, * sc in next ch-1 sp, ch 1; rep from * across, end with sc in last ch-sp, sc in 2nd ch of turning ch. Ch 1, turn.

Row 3: Sc in first sc, * ch 1, sc in next ch-1 sp; rep from * across, end with ch 1, sc in last sc.

Rep Rows 2 and 3 until same length as filet block. Fasten off.

Assembly: Beg with filet block in corner, arrange blocks in a 3-block x 3-block checkerboard pat. With right sides up, whipstitch blocks tog through front lps only.

Edging: Rnd 1: Right side facing, with afghan turned to work across long edge, join yarn in ch-1 sp after corner, work 2 sc in each sp of filet block, sc in each sc of solid block, work across filet block as before, work 4 sc in corner; to work across end, sc in each st across. Continue around afghan as established, join with sl st to first sc.

Rnd 2: Ch 5 for first tr and ch 1, * [sk 1 sc, tr in next sc, ch 1] to corner; in corner, sk first sc, [tr, ch 1] twice in each of next 2 sc; rep from * around as established. Join with sl st to 4th ch of starting ch-5.

Rnd 3: Ch 3 for first dc, dc in next ch-1 sp, dc in tr * [ch 3, sk 1 tr, dc in next tr, dc in ch-1 sp, dc in next tr] to corner; in corner, ch 3 and sk first tr in corner group, 2 dc in next tr, 2 dc in ch-1 sp, 2 dc in next tr; rep from * around as established. Join with sl st to top of starting ch-3.

Rnd 4: Sl st in top of next 2 dc, sl st in next ch, ch 3 for first dc, 2 dc in same ch-3 sp, * [ch 3, 3 dc in ch-3 sp]

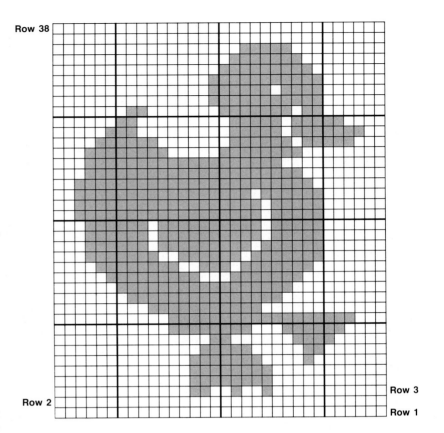

Row 38
Row 2
Row 3
Row 1

to corner; in corner, ch 3, sk first dc in corner group, 2 dc in next dc, 3 dc in next dc, 2 dc in next dc; rep from * around as established. Ch 3 and join with sl st to top of starting ch-3.

Rnd 5: Ch 5 for first tr and ch 1, [tr and ch 1 in same st] 3 times; * [tr, ch 1] 4 times in 2nd st of next dc group (tr cluster completed); rep from * to corner; in corner [sk 1 dc in corner group, tr cluster in next dc] 3 times, sk 1 dc; rep from * around, working corners as established. Join with sl st to 4th ch of starting ch-5.

Rnd 6: [Sc in next ch-1 sp, ch 4] 3 times, * sk ch-1 sp between tr clusters, [sc in next ch-1 sp, ch 4] 3 times; rep from * around. Join with sl st to first sc. Fasten off.

Finishing: Cut 2 (54″) lengths of ribbon and weave them through Rnd 2 of the edging at the ends of the afghan. Cut 2 (62″) lengths of ribbon and weave them through Rnd 2 of the edging at the sides of the afghan. Tie ribbons in bows at corners.

Floral Garland

Greet the season with an elegant garland of blossoms as soft as the first spring breeze. Join flower strips made of mohair yarn with blue-sky borders, and finish with scalloped edging.

MATERIALS

Yarn description: Worsted-weight mohair blend and sportweight wool blend.

Yarn pictured: (No longer available.) Welcomme® Super Mohair, 40-gr. balls, 5 Blue #108, 4 Green #109, 3 Rose #102, 1 Lavender #106, 1 Yellow #134; Pernelle® Touareg, 50-gr. balls, 5 Blue #211, 4 Green #217, 3 Rose #214, 1 Lavender #215, 1 Yellow #209.

TOOLS AND EQUIPMENT

Size J crochet hook; tapestry needle.

DIRECTIONS

Note: Afghan is worked with one strand each of mohair and Touareg in the same color held tog.

Dc cluster: Keeping last lp of each st on hook, work 4 dc in next st, yo and draw through 5 lps on hook (dc cluster completed).

Tr cluster: Keeping last lp of each st on hook, work 4 tr in next st, yo and draw through 5 lps on hook (tr cluster completed).

Center panel (make 1): Beg at center, with yellow, ch 145. Fasten off.

    Row 1: Join rose with sl st in first ch, * sk 3 ch, 8 tr in next ch, sk 3 ch, sl st in next ch; rep from * across; do not fasten off, turn piece, sl st in first ch on opposite side, rep from * across opposite side of ch = 18 8-tr clusters on each side (36 total). Fasten off.

Row 2: Right side facing, join green with sl st in first st, ch 4 for first tr, * ch 2, dc cluster in 3rd tr, ch 2, dc cluster in 6th tr, ch 2, tr cluster in sl st; rep from * across, end last rep with tr in last st. Fasten off. Rep row on opposite side of panel.

Rows 3 and 4: Right side facing, join blue, ch 3 for first dc, 2 dc in next ch-2 sp, * 3 dc in next ch-2 sp; rep from * across to last ch-2 sp, end with 2 dc in last ch-2 sp, dc in last st. Ch 3, turn. Dc in each dc across. Fasten off. Rep Rows 3 and 4 on rem side of panel.

Row 5: Right side facing, join lavender with sl st in first st, ch 3 for first dc, * ch 2, sk 3 sts, 5 dc in next st, sk 3 sts, dc in each of next 2 sts; rep from * across, end last rep with dc in last st. Fasten off. Rep row on rem side of panel.

Row 6: Right side facing, join yellow with sl st in first st, * 3 sc in ch-2 sp, ch 1, sc in 3rd dc of 5-dc group, ch 1, 3 sc in ch-2 sp, ch 1; rep from * across, end last rep with 2 sc in last ch-2 sp, sc in last st. Fasten off. Rep row on rem side of panel.

Row 7: Right side facing, join green with sl st in first st, ch 3 for first dc, * ch 2, dc cluster in ch-1 sp; rep from * across, end with ch 2, dc in last sc. Fasten off. Rep row on rem side of panel.

Row 8: Right side facing, join blue, ch 3 for first dc, 2 dc in next ch-sp, * 3 dc in next ch-2 sp; rep from * across, end with 2 dc in last ch-2 sp, dc in last st. Fasten off. Rep row on rem side of panel.

Row 9: Right side facing, join rose with sl st in first st, * sk 3 sts, 8 tr in next st, sk 3 sts, sl st in each of next 2 sts; rep from * across. Fasten off. Rep row on rem side of panel.

Row 10: With green, rep Row 2 on both sides of panel, working the tr cluster in 2nd sl st. Fasten off.

Rows 11 and 12: With blue, rep Rows 3 and 4 on both sides of panel. Fasten off.

Side panels (make 2): **Rows 1–9:** Rep center panel Rows 1–9.

Rows 10 and 11: Work center panel Rows 10 and 11 on one side of panel only, leaving rem side unworked. Fasten off.

Assembly: With blue Touareg, sew side panels to center panel along straight edges.

Edging: With 2 strands blue Toureg held tog as one, sc evenly across each end of afghan.

Confection in Chenille

FINISHED SIZE
Approximately 65" x 72".

MATERIALS
Yarn description: Acrylic chenille.
Yarn pictured: (No longer available.)
Neveda® Magic Chenille, 50-gr. balls, 18 Pink #6759 (main color, MC), 15 White #6761 (A), 12 Gold #6751 (B), 12 Cocoa #6753 (C).

TOOLS AND EQUIPMENT
Size J crochet hook, or size to obtain gauge.

GAUGE
3 dc = 1"
3 rows in pat st = 2"

DIRECTIONS
With A, ch 152.
　Row 1: Dc in 3rd ch from hook, and in each ch across = 151 dc including starting ch. Turn.
　Row 2: Ch 3 for first dc, * dc in each of next 3 dc, ch 1, sk 1 dc; rep from * across, end with 1 dc in each of last 2 dc, dc in top of starting ch. Fasten off. Turn.
　Row 3: Join MC with sl st in first st, ch 3 for first dc, yo and draw up a lp from st 2 rows below, complete as a dc (long dc completed), * dc in each of next 3 dc, long dc in next dc; rep from * across, end with dc in top of turning ch. Fasten off. Turn.
　Row 4: Join B, ch 3 for first dc, dc in each dc across. Turn.

Rep Rows 2–4 for pat until about 72" from beg, end with A; work pat in following color arrangement: for each Row 3 rep use MC. Use A, B, and C alternately, joining each one in sequence at the beg of the rep of Row 4.

Edging: Right side facing, with piece turned to work across long edge, join A, ch 2 for first hdc, hdc evenly to next corner. Fasten off. Rep for rem long edge.

For a look as rich and appealing as a raspberry torte, layer rows of plush chenille in confectionary colors. Use a long stitch in luscious pink to accent the simple design.

Frosted with Pink

Mohair in a soft puff stitch makes a cuddle-me-close afghan in shades of pink. Long narrow panels of mohair are edged with a glittering metallic yarn and laced together with satin ribbon.

FINISHED SIZE
Approximately 45″ x 60″, not including fringe.

MATERIALS
Yarn description: Mohair blend and size 10 crochet cotton with a metallic twist.

Yarn pictured: (No longer available; see suggested substitute below.) Scheepjeswol® Mohair, 50-gr. balls, 30 Pink; Berroco, Inc. Aurora, 40-gr. tubes, 2 Gold.

Substitute: For Scheepjeswol® Mohair, use Neveda® Parello in color of choice.

Other: Offray double-faced pink satin ribbon (¼″ wide), 40 yd.

TOOLS AND EQUIPMENT
Size K crochet hook, or size to obtain gauge.

GAUGE
1 puff st and 1 sc = 1″
Panel = 9″ wide

DIRECTIONS
Puff st: [Yo and draw up a ¼″ lp] 3 times in same st, yo and through all lps on hook (1 puff st completed).

Panel (make 5): With mohair, ch 22.

Row 1: Sc in 2nd ch from hook, sc in next ch, ch 1, sk 1 ch, sc in each of next 15 ch, ch 1, sk 1 ch, sc in each of last 2 ch. Ch 1, turn.

Row 2: Sc in each of first 2 sc, ch 1, sk ch-1 sp, sc in each of next 15 sc, ch 1, sk ch-1 sp, sc in each of last 2 sc. Ch 1, turn.

Row 3: Sc in each of first 2 sc, ch 1, sk ch-1 sp, * sc in next sc, puff st in next sc; rep from * 6 times more, sc in next sc, ch 1, sk ch-1 sp, sc in each of last 2 sc. Ch 1, turn.

Row 4: Sc in each of first 2 sc, ch 1, sk ch-1 sp, sc in each of next 15 sc and puff sts, ch 1, sk ch-1 sp, sc in each of last 2 sc. Ch 1, turn.

Rep Rows 3 and 4 until there are 70 rows of puff st. End by working Row 2 twice more. Fasten off.

Finishing: Cut strands of metallic yarn 14″ longer than panel. Weave 8 strands held tog through the ch-1 sps on each side of each panel. Knot at ends of panel to secure.

Assembly: To join panels tog, lace 2 pieces of ribbon in crisscross pat through the sc edge of each panel, like lacing shoes (see photograph). Be sure to keep ribbons flat. Leave a tail approximately 7″ long at each end of afghan to match fringe. Tack ribbons to afghan at ends to secure.

Fringe: Knot 1 (14″) strand of mohair through each sc on ends of afghan. Trim mohair, ribbon, and metallic yarn even.

Spring Lambs

When spring lambs come out to play, there's always a maverick in the crowd!

FINISHED SIZE
Afghan: approximately 44" x 60".
Pillow: approximately 20" square.

MATERIALS
Yarn description: Worsted-weight acrylic.

Yarn pictured: (One color is no longer available; see suggested substitute below.) National Yarn Crafts Natura® Wintuk (a DuPont certification mark), 4-oz. skeins, 14 Off-White (color A); 2 each Coffee (B), Cashmere (C); 1 each Black, Avocado; a few yd. each Blue Jewel, White.

Substitute: For Avocado, use Paddy Green.

Other: 17" pillow form.

TOOLS AND EQUIPMENT
Size J crochet hook, or size to obtain gauge; white tissue paper; tapestry needle.

GAUGE
13 sts = 4"

DIRECTIONS
Afghan: Panel (make 3): With A, ch 144.

Row 1: Sc in 2nd ch from hook and in each ch across = 143 sc total. Ch 1, turn.

Row 2: Sc in each sc across. Ch 1 and turn.

Rep Row 2 until 20" from beg.

Embroidery: Cut 3 pieces of white tissue paper, each 20" x 44". Enlarge sheep pat. Transfer sheep pat to each piece of tissue paper 3 times; refer to photograph for placement. Sheep on top and bottom panels should face in one direction; those on middle panel should face in opposite direction. Notice that sheep are very close tog; measurement of 3 sheep should total 42".

Baste paper pats to crocheted panels and embroider through paper. Use coffee and chain stitch for all outlines and nostrils; use white long stitch for pupil of eye and surround pupil with blue long stitch; fill in outside of ears and legs with coffee and chain stitch (follow the direction of the arrows); use fly stitch and cashmere for body and head of sheep (refer to photograph for variations in individual sheep). Remember to embroider 1 black sheep (substitute black for cashmere and coffee). When embroidery is completed, tear paper away from panel and tease from under embroidery.

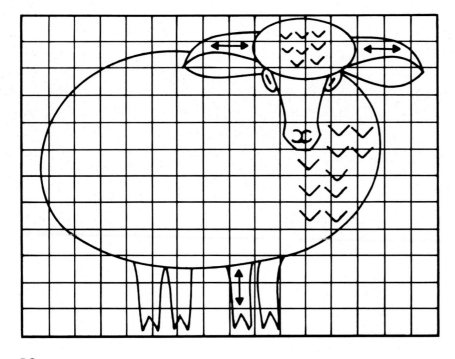

Each square = 1".

Assembly: Right sides facing, matching long edges, whipstitch panels tog.

Use these seams as base lines to embroider grass with long st (see photograph for placement).

Edging: Rnd 1: Join A in any corner, * 3 sc in corner, sc evenly to next corner; rep from * 3 times more, join with sl st to first sc.

Rnd 2: Ch 1, sc in each sc around, work 3 sc in each corner. Join with sl st to first sc. Fasten off.

Rnds 3 and 4: Join C and rep Rnd 2. At end of Rnd 4, fasten off.

Rnds 5 and 6: Join B and rep Rnd 2. At end of Rnd 6, fasten off.

Pillow: Square (make 2): With A, ch 57.

Row 1: Sc in 2nd ch from hook and in each ch across = 56 sc. Ch 1 and turn.

Row 2: Sc in each sc across. Ch 1 and turn.

Rep Row 2 until 17" from beg. Fasten off.

Embroidery: Enlarge sheep pat and transfer to a 17" square of tissue paper. Baste paper pat to one pillow piece and embroider as for afghan.

Assembly: With wrong sides facing, sc pillow pieces tog around 3 sides. Insert pillow form and sc last side tog.

Edging: Rnd 1: Join A in any corner, * 3 sc in corner, sc evenly to next corner; rep from * 3 times more, join with sl st to first sc.

Rnd 2: Ch 1, sc in each sc around, work 3 sc in each corner. Join with sl st to first sc. Fasten off.

Rnds 3 and 4: Join C and rep Rnd 2. At end of Rnd 4, fasten off.

Rnds 5 and 6: Join B and rep Rnd 2. At end of Rnd 6, fasten off.

Pastel Medallions

Spring blooms again in soft shades of blue, green, pink, lilac, and yellow in this pretty pastel afghan. This design works up quickly and easily in rounds of double crochet.

FINISHED SIZE
Approximately 48" x 78".

MATERIALS
Yarn description: Worsted-weight acrylic.
Yarn pictured: (No longer available; see suggested substitute below.) Reynolds Reynelle®, 3½-oz. skeins, 8 White #9001, 1 each Coral #9039, Baby Green #9003, Alpine #9025, Colonial Blue #9047, Jonquil #9011, Horizon Blue #9046, Light Lime #9055, Medium Pink #9075, Lilac #9053.

Substitute: Reynolds Deluxe Reynelle®, White #8060, Coral #8073, Baby Green #8028, Mauve #8071, Cornflower #8016, Baby Yellow #8038, Baby Blue #8019, Sea Green #8026, Medium Pink #8081, Lilac #8009.

TOOLS AND EQUIPMENT
Size G crochet hook, or size to obtain gauge.

GAUGE
Motif = 2", not including lps

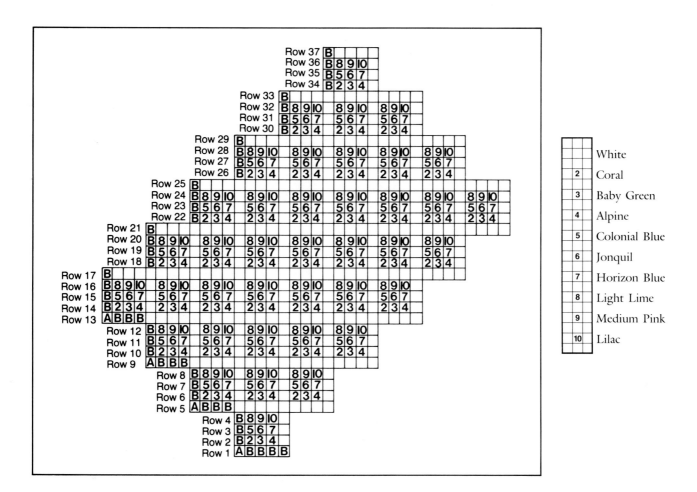

The color key (right side of diagram):

		White
2		Coral
3		Baby Green
4		Alpine
5		Colonial Blue
6		Jonquil
7		Horizon Blue
8		Light Lime
9		Medium Pink
10		Lilac

DIRECTIONS

Note: Afghan is worked on the diagonal and motifs are joined while working. The letters in the diagram indicate which motif to use. Motif A is always white and is worked as an individual unit. Motif B is joined to previous motifs on one or two sides, depending on position in diagram. Numbers in diagram indicate color of each motif; where there is no number use white.

Motif A: With white, ch 6 and join with sl st to form a ring.

Rnd 1: Ch 7, sl st in 4th ch from hook (corner lp completed); * work 6 dc in ring, ch 4, sl st in top of last dc; rep from * twice more; end with 5 dc in ring, join with sl st to 3rd ch of starting ch-7 (first motif of Row 1 of diagram completed). Fasten off.

Motif B: With white, ch 6 and join with sl st to form a ring.

Rnd 1: Ch 5, sl st in corner lp on previous motif, ch 2, sl st in 2nd ch of ch-5 (2 corner lps joined), 3 dc in ring, sl st in center of corresponding 6-dc group on previous motif (motifs joined at center), 3 dc in ring of second motif, ch 2, sl st in corresponding corner lp of previous motif, ch 2, sl st in top of dc of second motif (2 motifs joined along side), complete rem 3 sides as for motif A (2nd motif of Row 1 of diagram completed). Fasten off.

Complete Row 1 of chart with white and motif B.

Row 2: Beg with motif B in white. Continue with motif B and follow color key.

Rows 3–37: Following diagram and color key, continue to make and join motifs.

Lace & Lavender

FINISHED SIZE
Approximately 40″ x 60″, not including lace ruffle.

MATERIALS
Yarn description: Sportweight cotton and pearl cotton.
Yarn pictured: White sportweight cotton, 2-oz. skeins, 10 White; DMC® Pearl Cotton, size 5, 12 balls Lilac #554 (color A), 12 balls Medium Purple #553 (B), 24 skeins Deep Purple #550 (C).
Other: Cotton-blend lace insertion (2″ wide), 5½ yd.; cotton-blend lace edging (2″ wide), 12 yd.; craft glue.

TOOLS AND EQUIPMENT
Size F crochet hook, or size to obtain gauge; tapestry needle.

GAUGE
9 sc = 2″
5 dc = 1″

DIRECTIONS
Cut 5 (40″) lengths of lace insertion. Fold ½″ on each end of lace to wrong side and glue in place. Allow glue to dry before starting crochet.

Row 1: Right side of lace insertion facing, with lace turned to work across long edge, using 1 strand each white and A held tog as one, join yarn in corner and work 163 sc evenly spaced to next corner (9 sc to 2″). Turn.

Row 2: Ch 3 for first dc, dc in each sc across. Turn.

Rows 3–5: Ch 3 for first dc, dc in each dc across. Turn. At end of Row 5, fasten off A.

Row 6: With white only, sc in each dc across. Turn.

Row 7: Join B, and working with white and B held tog as one, ch 3 for first dc, dc in each sc across. Turn.

Rows 8–10: Ch 3 for first dc, dc in each dc across. Turn. At end of Row 10, fasten off B.

Row 11: Rep Row 6.

Row 12: Join C and rep Row 7.

Row 13: Rep Row 8. Fasten off.
Rep Rows 1–13 on opposite edge of lace insertion.

Rep Rows 1–13 on both sides of each piece of lace insertion.

Assembly: Lay panels with right sides up and Row 13s tog; whipstitch panels tog with white yarn.

Edging: Rnd 1: Right side facing, join white in corner, * 3 sc in corner, sc evenly to next corner; rep from * around. Join with sl st to first sc.

Rnds 2 and 3: Sc in each sc around, working 3 sc in each corner, join with sl st to first sc. At the end of Rnd 3, fasten off.

Finishing: Sew lace edging to the last sc edging rnd. Tack ends of lace tog where they meet.

Frills and finery—with no fuss! Hold white cotton yarn and lavender pearl cotton together as you stitch, for bands of color as delicate as a springtime bouquet. Use purchased lace inserts to join the crocheted panels, and finish with a lacy ruffle.

Flower Cart Afghan

You can arrange a cascade of color on our old-fashioned flower cart. Choose cool spring pastels or heady summer brights and combine them with the technique called intarsia. Wind each color of yarn on a separate bobbin and twist strands at color changes to interlock.

FINISHED SIZE
Approximately 52″ x 66″.

MATERIALS
Yarn description: Worsted-weight acrylic.
Yarn pictured: (No longer available; see suggested substitute below.) Columbia-Minerva® Nantuck®, 24 oz. Light Rose (color LR), 12 oz. White (W), 8 oz. Raspberry (R), 4 oz. each of Gray (G), Baby Pink, Light Yellow, Tangerine, Forest Green, Leaf Green, Sapphire, Baby Blue.
Substitute: Columbia-Minerva® Windspun™ or Nantuck Brushed™ in colors of choice.

TOOLS AND EQUIPMENT
Size G afghan hook (22″ long); size G crochet hook; bobbins.

DIRECTIONS
Note: When working the chart in afghan st, work across row, drawing up lps in color indicated; work lps off by using same color as lp on hook. To avoid holes, bring up new color from under dropped color. Changing colors is easier if yarn is wound on bobbins.

If a color is to be used again in 4 sts or less, work over it with the next few sts and pick it up when needed. If a color is not needed for more than 4 sts, drop it to the wrong side of work and pick up when needed. Fasten off each color when no longer needed.

Afghan st: Row 1: *Step 1:* Keeping all lps on hook, draw up a lp through top lp only, in 2nd ch from hook and each ch across = same number of lps as chs. Do not turn.
Step 2: Yo and draw through first lp on hook, * yo and through 2 lps on hook; rep from * across (1 lp rem on hook for the first lp of next row). Do not turn.
Row 2: *Step 1:* Keeping all lps on hook, draw up a lp from under 2nd vertical bar, * draw up a lp from under next vertical bar; rep from * across. Do not turn.
Step 2: Rep Step 2 of Row 1.
Rep both steps of Row 2 for number of afghan st rows specified.
Note: Both steps of afghan st (see Row 2 above) equal 1 row on the chart. Read chart right to left for Step 1 and left to right for Step 2.

Afghan: With afghan hook and LR, ch 168.
Row 1: Work both steps of Row 1 of afghan st in LR (Row 1 of chart completed).
Row 2: Following Row 2 of chart and working Row 2, Step 1 of afghan st, draw up 5 lps LR (*Note:* With lp rem from previous row, there will be 6 LR lps on hook), drop LR, with W draw up 25 lps, drop W, with LR draw up 15 lps, with W draw up 15 lps; continue across row of chart as established. End by rep Row 2, Step 2 of afghan st.

Continue following chart as established, making color changes as described above. To work the flowers, use colors as desired (see photograph). For the colors we chose, see Materials: baby pink, etc. Fasten off after last row of chart by working a sl st in each vertical bar across.

Ruffle edging: Rnd 1: Right side facing, with crochet hook, join W in any corner, ch 1, work 3 sc in same corner, * sc evenly to next corner, 3 sc in corner; rep from * twice more, sc evenly across last edge. Join with sl st to first sc. Ch 1, turn.

Rnd 2: * [Sc in next sc, ch 1, sk 1 sc] to next corner, 3 sc in corner; rep from * around as established. Join with sl st to first sc. Turn.

Rnd 3: Sl st to next ch-1 sp, ch 4 for first dc and ch 1, * [in next ch-1 sp work dc and ch 1] to corner, [dc and ch 1] in each sc at corner; rep from * around as established. Join with sl st to 3rd ch of starting ch. Turn.

Rnds 4–6: Sl st to next ch-1 sp, ch 5 for first dc and ch 2, * [in next ch-sp work dc and ch 2] to corner, in each ch-sp at corner work dc, ch 2, and dc; rep from * around as established. Join with sl st to 3rd ch of starting ch. Do not turn. At end of Rnd 6, fasten off.

Rnd 7: Join LR in ch-sp at center of any corner, ch 8 for first dc and ch 5, [dc, ch 5] in each ch-sp around. Join with sl st to 3rd ch of starting ch. Fasten off.

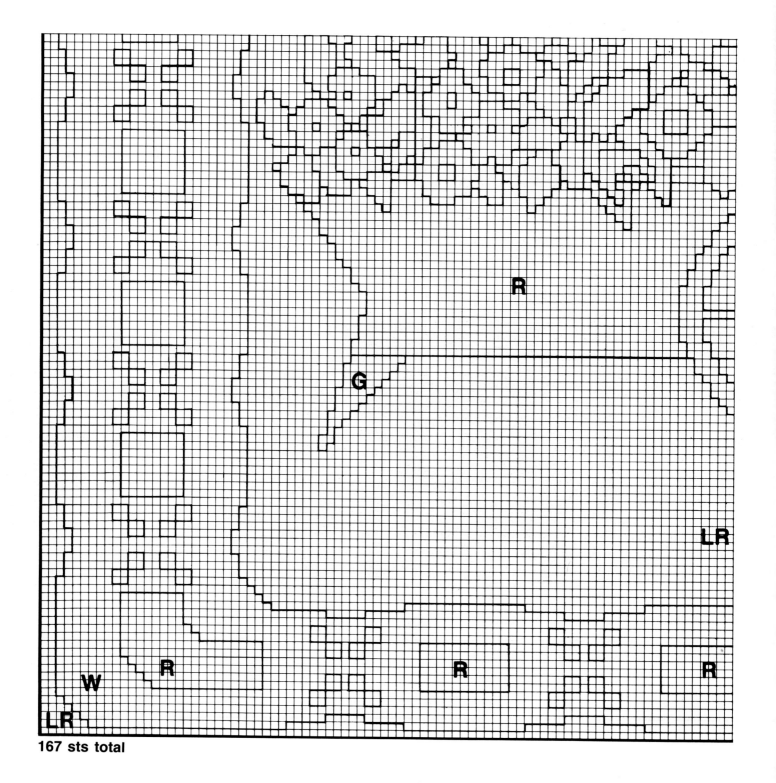

167 sts total

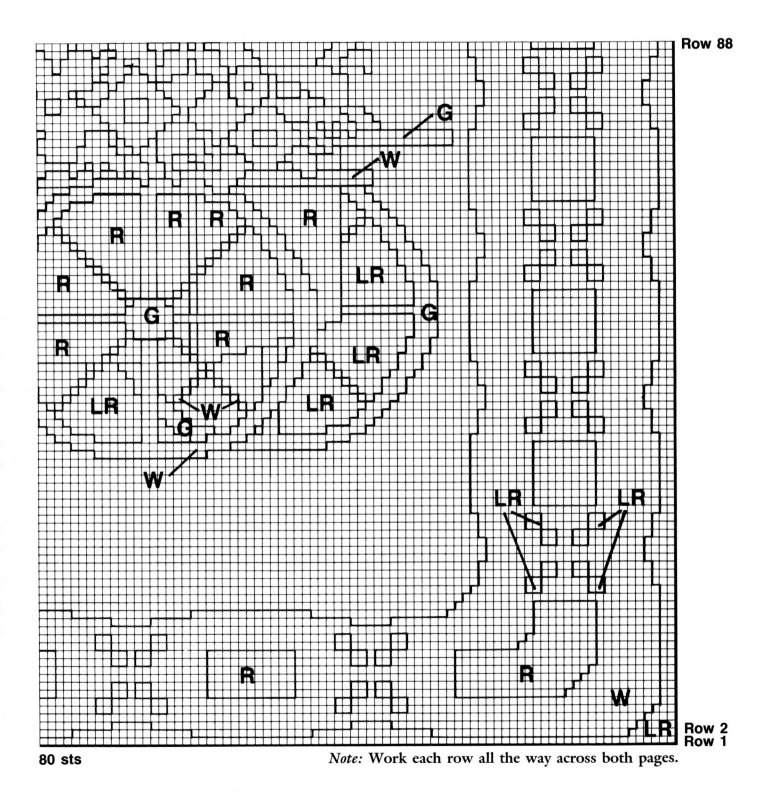

Row 88

G

W

R R R R

R

R LR

R G

G

R

R LR

LR

LR W

G

LR

W

LR LR

R R

W

80 sts

LR

Row 2

Row 1

Note: Work each row all the way across both pages.

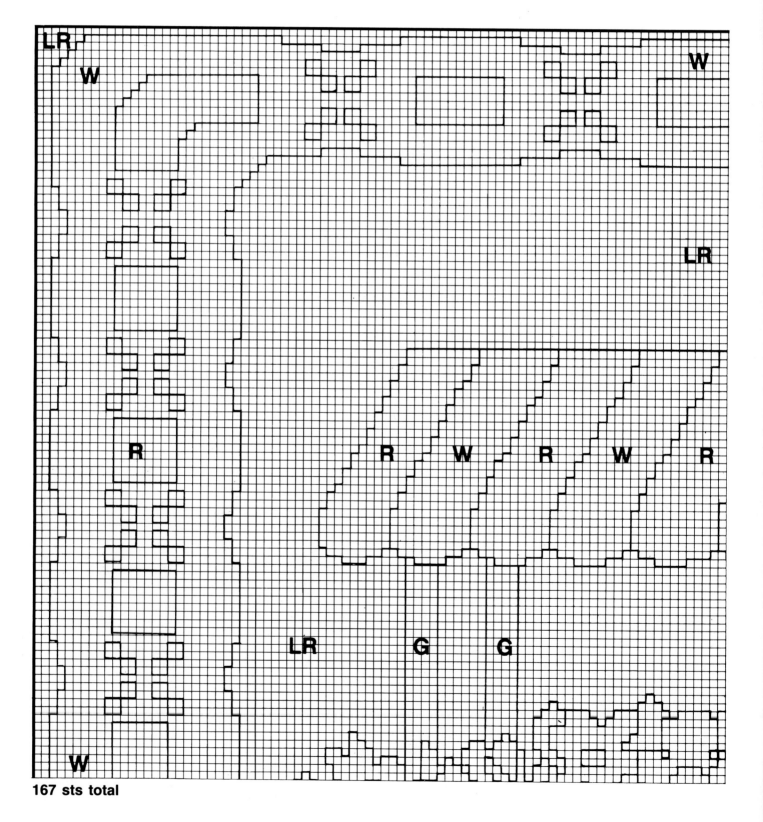

167 sts total

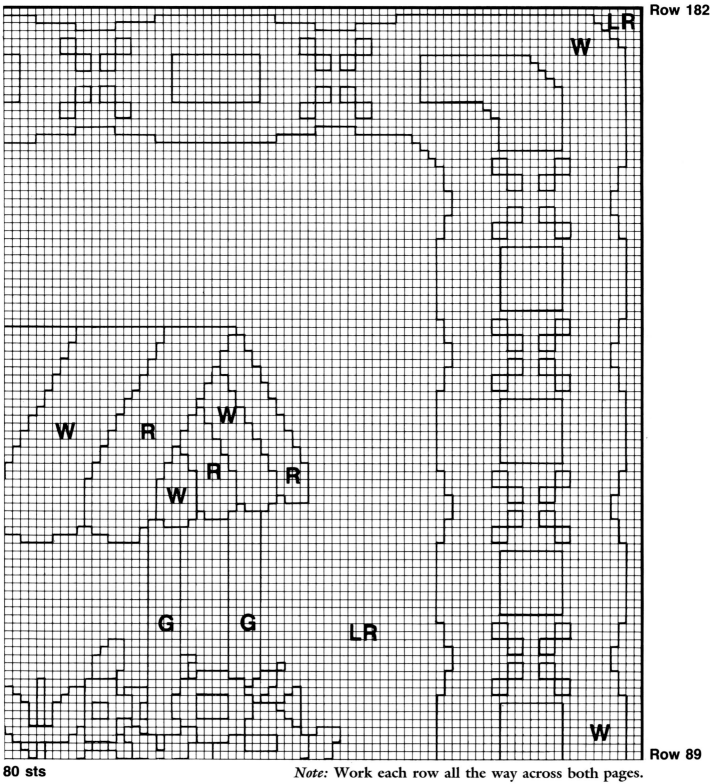

80 sts

Note: Work each row all the way across both pages.

Peach Delight

Borrow a trick or two from your quilting friends to make this "pieceful" coverlet for baby. Cream blocks alternate with peach-and-cream patchwork in a traditional chain pattern.

FINISHED SIZE
Approximately 40″ square.

MATERIALS
Yarn description: Worsted-weight cotton.
Yarn pictured: Lily® Sugar and Cream®, 2½-oz. skeins, 12 White, 4 Peach.

TOOLS AND EQUIPMENT
Size F crochet hook, or size to obtain gauge; tapestry needle.

GAUGE
4 sc = 1″, 5 rows = 1″

DIRECTIONS
Solid block (make 12): With white, ch 31.
Row 1: Sc in 2nd ch from hook and in each ch across = 30 sc. Ch 1 and turn.
Row 2: Sc in each sc across row. Ch 1, turn.
Rep Row 2 until 34 rows from beg. Fasten off.

Pieced block (make 13):
Small square (make 6 white and 9 peach for each block): Ch 7.
Row 1: Sc in 2nd ch from hook and in each ch across = 6 sc. Ch 1 and turn.
Row 2: Sc in each sc across row. Ch 1, turn.
Rep Row 2 until 6 rows from beg. Fasten off.
Small rectangle (SR) (make 2 for each block): With white, ch 13.
Row 1: Sc in 2nd ch from hook and in each ch across = 12 sc. Ch 1 and turn.
Row 2: Sc in each sc across row. Ch 1, turn.
Rep Row 2 until 6 rows from beg. Fasten off.
Large rectangle (LR) (make 2 for each block): With white, ch 19.
Row 1: Sc in 2nd ch from hook and in each ch across = 18 sc. Ch 1 and turn.
Row 2: Sc in each sc across row. Ch 1, turn.
Rep Row 2 until 6 rows from beg. Fasten off.

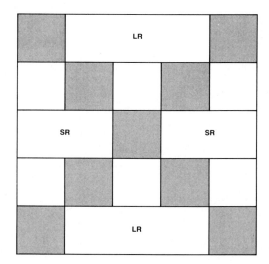

Assembly: Referring to diagram and working with wrong sides facing, sew squares and rectangles tog to form pieced blocks.
Beg with a pieced block in corner, arrange blocks in a 5-block x 5-block checkerboard pat. With right sides up, whipstitch blocks tog through back lps only, with white yarn.

Edging: Rnd 1: Join white in any corner, work * sc, ch 1, and sc in corner, [ch 1, sk 1 st, sc in next sc] to next corner, ch 1; rep from * around as established. Join with sl st to first sc.

Rnd 2: Sl st to ch-1 corner, ch 6 for first dc and ch 3, dc in same corner, * [ch 1, dc in next ch-1 sp] to next corner, ch 1, in corner work dc, ch 3, and dc; rep from * around as established, join with sl st to 3rd ch of starting ch.

Rnd 3: Sl st to ch-3 corner, ch 6 for first dc and ch 3, dc in same corner, * [ch 1, dc in next ch-1 sp] to next corner, ch 1, in corner work dc, ch 3, and dc; rep from * around as established, join with sl st to 3rd ch of starting ch.

Rnd 4: Sl st to ch-3 corner, in corner work 2 sc, ch 1, and 2 sc, * [sc in next ch-1 sp, ch 1] twice, ch 7, sk 2 ch-1 sp; rep from * to next corner adjusting as necessary to end with sc before corner, in corner work 2 sc, ch 1, and 2 sc; rep from * around as established, join with sl st to first sc.

Rnd 5: Sl st to ch-2 corner, * in corner work 2 sc, ch 1, and 2 sc, ** sc evenly to next ch-7 sp, in ch-7 work sc, 2 hdc, dc, 2 hdc, sc; rep from ** to next corner, sc in sc before corner; rep from * around as established, join with sl st to first sc.

Rnd 6: Sl st to ch-2 corner, * in corner work 2 sc, ch 1, and 2 sc, ** sc in each sc, hdc in each hdc, dc in each dc, hdc in each hdc; rep from ** to next corner; rep from * around as established, join with sl st to first sc. Fasten off.

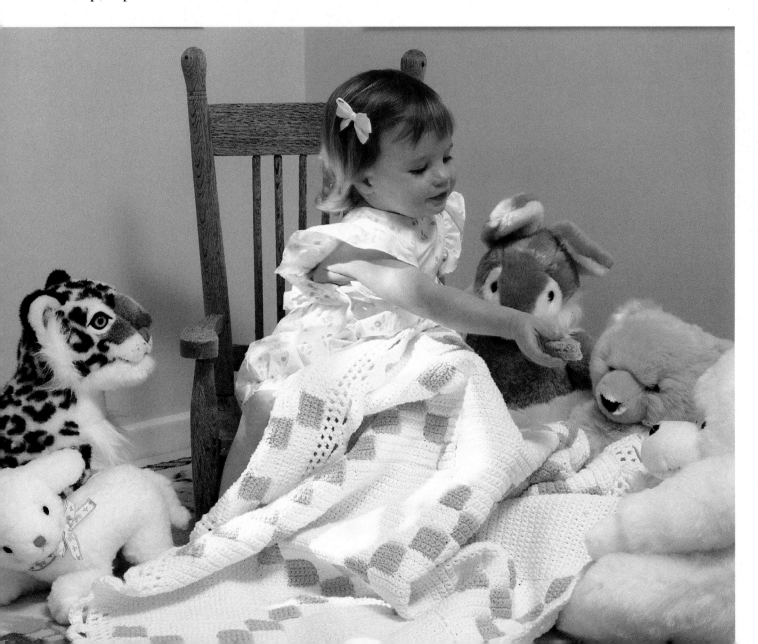

Blossoms on a Trellis

A "bit o' the Irish" is the key to this afghan's lacy charm. Filet crochet panels feature blossoms trimmed with raised single stitches, a simplified technique in the style of Irish crochet.

FINISHED SIZE
Approximately 66" x 74".

MATERIALS
Yarn description: Worsted-weight acrylic.
Yarn pictured: (No longer available; see suggested substitute below.) Talon American Dawn Odyssey, 3½-oz. skeins, 15 White, 4 Gray, 3 Pink.
Substitute: Caron® Wintuk (a DuPont certification mark) in colors of choice.

TOOLS AND EQUIPMENT
Size H crochet hook, or size to obtain gauge; bobbins.

GAUGE
4 sc = 1"

DIRECTIONS
Note: To avoid holes when changing colors, bring up new color from under dropped color. Always bring up new color as last yo of old color.

When working jacquard chart, carry color not in use across the row by working over it.

When working filet chart, wind several bobbins of pink. Do not carry pink across the row; drop the bobbin to the back of the work when not in use and pick up when needed on the return row. Carry white across the row by working over it.

Afghan: With gray, ch 298.

Row 1: Sc in 2nd ch from hook and in each ch across = 297 sc. Ch 1 and turn (Row 1 of jacquard chart completed).

Row 2: Sc in each sc across; on last sc, with white, work yo and draw through 2 lps on hook. With white, ch 1, turn.

Row 3: With white, draw up a lp in first st, with gray, work yo and through both lps on hook (color change completed), changing colors as before, work * 1 gray sc, 5 white sc; rep from * across, end with 1 gray sc, 1 white sc; on last st work yo with gray (Row 3 of jacquard chart completed). With gray, ch 1, turn.

Rows 4–18: Continue following jacquard chart as established, rep indicated portion of chart for pat.

Row 19: Sc in each sc across, work 2 sc in last sc = 298 sc. Fasten off. Turn.

Row 20: With white, sc in each sc across. Turn.

Row 21: Ch 6 for first dc and ch 2, sk 2 sc, * dc in next sc, ch 2, sk 2 sc; rep from * across, end with dc in last sc. Turn.

Row 22: * Sc in dc, 2 sc in ch-2 sp; rep from * across, end with sc in 3rd ch of starting ch-6 of previous row. Turn.

Row 23: Rep Row 21.

Row 24: Ch 6 for first dc and ch 2, [dc in next dc, ch 2] 13 times, ch 2, with pink work dc in next dc, 2 dc in ch-2 sp, dc in next dc (filled mesh completed), with white ch 2, dc in next dc, ch 2; continue in pat, rep indicated

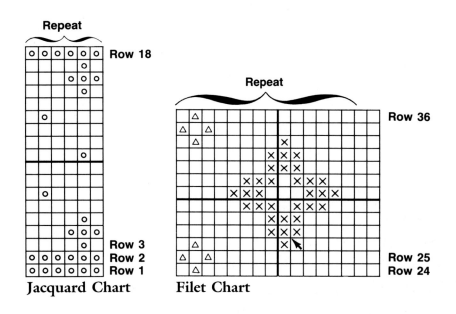

Jacquard Chart   **Filet Chart**

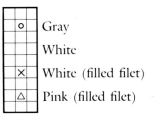

	Gray
	White
×	White (filled filet)
△	Pink (filled filet)

portion of filet chart (Row 24 of filet chart completed). Turn.

Rows 25–36: Continue following filet chart as established. (*Note:* To work open mesh over filled mesh, ch 2, sk 2 dc, dc in next dc.)

Row 37: Rep Row 21.
Row 38: Rep Row 22.
Row 39: Rep Row 21.
Row 40: Rep Row 22.
Row 41: Join gray, sc in each sc across to last 2 sc, draw up a lp in each of last 2 sts, yo and through 3 lps on hook (1 sc dec completed).

Rep Rows 2–41 following charts as established until there are 4 strips filet pat and 5 strips jacquard pat; end last rep with 2 rows gray = Rows 18 and 19. Fasten off.

Edging: Join white in corner and work 1 row sc across each end of afghan. Join gray in corner and work 1 row sc across each side edge of afghan.

Irish crochet: With right side of afghan facing, join pink at point indicated on filet chart. Working around each post, work 1 row sc around white filled-filet design; work 3 sc in each corner. To end, join with sl st to first sc and fasten off. Rep for each white filled-filet design.

Summer

Embossed Afghans

This elegant pair echoes the intriguing textures you might find in an Italian cathedral or palazzo. With your crochet hook, you can sculpt those textures in tones of white, creating subtle shadows.

Venetian Dome

FINISHED SIZE
Approximately 50" x 63".

MATERIALS
Yarn description: Worsted-weight acrylic.
Yarn pictured: National Yarn Crafts Natura® Wintuk (a DuPont certification mark), made from DuPont's Orlon® acrylic fibers, 3½-oz. skeins, 12 each White, Eggshell.

TOOLS AND EQUIPMENT
Size K crochet hook, or size to obtain gauge; tapestry needle.

GAUGE
Square = 4½"

DIRECTIONS
Square (make 154): With white, ch 4 and join with sl st to form a ring.

Rnd 1: Ch 2 for first hdc, work 2 hdc in ring, ch 1 for corner, [3 hdc in ring, ch 1 for corner] 3 times, join with sl st to top of starting ch (4 corners established).

Rnd 2: Ch 1, sc in top of starting ch and in each of next 2 hdc, 3 sc in ch-1 sp for corner, [sc in each of next 3 hdc, 3 sc in ch-1 sp for corner] 3 times, join with sl st to first sc.

Rnd 3: Ch 1, sc in same sc as sl st, sc in each of next 3 sc, 3 sc in next sc for corner, [sc in each of next 5 sc, 3 sc in next sc for corner] 3 times, sc in last sc, join with sl st to first sc = 7 sc between corner sts on each edge.

Rnd 4: Ch 1, sc in same sc as sl st, sc in each of next 5 sc, 3 sc in next sc for corner, [sc in each of next 7 sc, 3 sc in next sc for corner] 3 times, sc in last sc, join with sl st to first sc.

Rnd 5: Ch 1, sc in same sc as sl st, sc in each of next 6 sc, 3 sc in next sc for corner, [sc in each of next 9 sc, 3 sc in next sc for corner] 3 times, sc in last sc, join with sl st to first sc = 11 sc between corner sts on each edge. Fasten off.

Rnd 6: Sk center 3 sc at corner, join eggshell with sl st in next sc, sc in same st as sl st, * work hdc around post of st 2 rows below (long hdc completed), work long dc around post of st 3 rows below, long tr around post of st 4 rows below, long dtr around post of hdc on Rnd 1, long tr around post of st 4 rows below, long dc around post of st 3 rows below, long hdc around post of st 2 rows below, sc in next sc immediately before 3 sc corner, sc in next sc, 3 sc in next sc for corner, sc in each of next 2 sc; rep from * 3 times more, end with sc in last sc, join with sl st to first sc.

Rnd 7: Ch 1, * sc evenly to next corner, 3 sc in center sc of corner; rep from * 3 times more, sc in last sc, join with sl st to first sc. Fasten off.

Assembly: Afghan will be 11 squares wide and 14 squares long. With right sides facing, whipstitch squares tog through inner lps only.

Edging: Rnd 1: Join white in any corner, * work 3 sc in corner, sc evenly to next corner; rep from * around, join with sl st to first sc and fasten off.

Rnd 2: Join eggshell and, working from left to right, work a rnd of reverse sc around entire afghan (do not inc at corners). Join with sl st to first sc and fasten off.

Tassels (make 4): Hold eggshell and white tog as one, and wind around a 7″ length of cardboard 40 times. At one end, slip a piece of yarn under the lps and tie. Cut other end. Tie another piece of yarn tightly around strands about 1″ below tied end. Sew a tassel to each corner of afghan.

Florentine Frieze

FINISHED SIZE
Approximately 50" x 70".

MATERIALS
Yarn description: Worsted-weight acrylic.
Yarn pictured: National Yarn Crafts Natura® Wintuk (a DuPont certification mark), made from Dupont's Orlon® acrylic fibers, 3½-oz. skeins, 12 Eggshell, 9 White.

TOOLS AND EQUIPMENT
Size K crochet hook, or size to obtain gauge; tapestry needle.

GAUGE
Square = 7"

DIRECTIONS
Square (make 70): With eggshell, ch 5 and join with sl st to form a ring.

　　Rnd 1: Work 16 sc in ring, join with sl st to first sc.

　　Rnd 2: Ch 1, sc in same sc as sl st,

in next sc [yo and draw up a lp, yo and through 2 lps on hook] 3 times, yo and through 4 lps on hook (bobble st completed), * sc in next sc, bobble st in next sc; rep from * around, join with sl st to back lp of first sc = 8 bobbles around.

Rnd 3: Ch 1, working in back lps only, sc in same st as sl st, * 3 sc in bobble st (corner completed), sc in each of next 3 sts; rep from * 3 times more, end with sc in last 2 sts, join with sl st to first sc. Fasten off.

Rnd 4: Join white in back lp of same st as sl st, sc in next sc, * 3 sc in next sc for corner, sc in each of next 5 sc; rep from * 3 times more, end with sc in last 3 sts, join to back lp of first sc.

Rnd 5: Ch 1, sc in back lp of same st as sl st, dc in front lp of st 2 rows below, sc in back lp of next st, * in corner sc work [sc in back lp, dc in front lp of st 2 rows below, sc in back lp (all in one st)], [sc in back lp of next sc, dc in front lp of st 2 rows below] 3 times, sc in back lp of next st; rep from * 3 times more, end with [sc in back lp of next sc, dc in front lp of st 2 rows below] twice, join with sl st to first sc. Fasten off.

Rnd 6: Join eggshell in back lp of same st as sl st and, working in back lps only, sc around, work 3 sc in each corner dc. At end of rnd, join with sl st to first sc = 11 sc between corner sts on each edge; 48 sc around. Fasten off.

Rnd 7: Join white in back lp of same st as sl st, ch 1, [dc in front lp of st 2 rows below, sc in back lp of next sc] to center corner st, * in corner sc work [dc in front lp of st 2 rows below, sc in back lp, dc in same front lp of st 2 rows below, sc in back lp, dc in same front lp of st 2 rows below (3 dc in front lp of center corner sc)], [sc in back lp of next st, dc in front lp of st 2 rows below] to st before next corner, sc in back lp of next st; rep from * around 3 times more, end with sc in back lp of last st, join with sl st to first st. Fasten off.

Rnd 8: Join eggshell in same st as sl st and, working in back lps only, sc around, work 3 sc in each corner. At end of rnd, join with sl st to first sc = 13 sc between corner sts on each edge; 56 sc around.

Rnd 9: Working in back lps only, sc in each sc around, work 3 sc in each corner. At end of rnd, join with sl st to first sc = 15 sc between corner sts on each edge; 64 sc around. Fasten off.

Rnd 10: Join white in same st as sl st, ch 1, sc in same st, [dc in front lp of sc 2 rows below, sc in back lp of next st] to center corner st, * in corner sc work [dc in front lp of st 2 rows below, sc in back lp, dc in same front lp of st 2 rows below, sc in back lp, dc in same front lp of st 2 rows below (3 dc in front lp of center corner sc)], [sc in back lp of next st, dc in front lp of sc 2 rows below] to st before next corner, sc in back lp of next st; rep from * 3 times more, end with sc in back lp of last st, join with sl st to first sc. Fasten off.

Rnd 11: Join eggshell in same st as sl st and, working in back lps only, sc in each st around, work 3 sc in each corner. Join with sl st to first sc and fasten off.

Assembly: Afghan will be 7 squares wide and 10 squares long. With right sides facing, whipstitch squares tog through inner lps only.

Edging: Rnd 1: Join eggshell in any corner and, working from left to right, work a rnd of reverse sc around entire afghan (do not inc at corners). Join with sl st to first sc. Fasten off.

Tassels (make 4): Wind eggshell around a 7″ length of cardboard 80 times. At one end, slip a piece of yarn under the lps and tie. Cut other end. Tie another piece of yarn tightly around strands about 1″ below tied end. Sew a tassel to each corner of afghan.

Butterflies

Cotton-blend chenille in airy filet crochet makes a lightweight throw that's perfect for easy summer living. Make it in sunny peach as an inviting accent for picnic or poolside.

FINISHED SIZE
Approximately 43" x 58".

MATERIALS
Yarn description: Chenille.
Yarn pictured: Patons Cotton Sahara, 1¾-oz. skeins, 15 Peach #2321.

TOOLS AND EQUIPMENT
Size F crochet hook, or size to obtain gauge.

GAUGE
9 dc = 2", 2 rows = 1"

DIRECTIONS
Panels (make 2): Ch 89 loosely.

Row 1: Dc in 3rd ch from hook and in each ch across = 88 dc including starting ch. Row 1 of chart (29 filled mesh) completed. Turn.

Row 2: Ch 3 for first dc, dc in each of next 6 dc, * ch 2, sk 2 dc, dc in next dc (open mesh over filled mesh completed), dc in each of next 9 dc; rep from * 5 times more; ch 2, sk 2 dc, dc in each of last 7 dc (Row 2 of chart completed). Turn.

Row 3: Ch 3 for first dc, dc in each of next 3 dc; * ch 2, sk 2 dc, dc in next dc, 2 dc in ch-2 sp, dc in next dc (filled mesh over open mesh completed); ch 2, sk 2 dc, dc in each of next 4 dc; rep from * 6 times more. Turn.

Rows 4–29: Continue following chart as established. At the end of Row 29, do not fasten off.

Rep Rows 1–29 of chart 3 times more to make a panel of 4 butterfly blocks. Fasten off.

Border: With right side facing and panel turned to work across long edge, join yarn in corner and work 2 sc in each dc post to next corner. Fasten off. Rep for rem long edge of panel.

Assembly: With butterflies facing in the same direction, lay panels right side up, join yarn with sc in corner of first panel, ch 1, sc in corner of 2nd panel, * ch 1, sk 1 sc on panel 1, sc in next st, ch 1, sk 1 sc on panel 2, sc in next st; rep from * across as established to join the 2 panels; end with last sts in corner of each panel.

Edging: Row 1: With right side facing and afghan turned to work across long edge, join yarn in corner, * ch 3, sk next st, sc in next st; rep from * to next corner, ending with last sc in corner. Turn.

Row 2: Ch 3 for first dc, dc in next ch-3 lp, * ch 1, dc in next ch-3 lp; rep

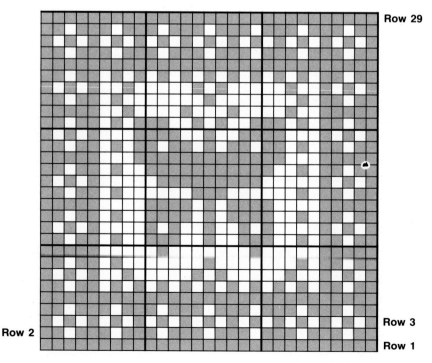

Row 29

Row 2

Row 3

Row 1

from * across, end with dc in last sc. Turn.

Row 3: Sc in top of turning ch, sc in each ch-1 and dc across. Fasten off.

Rep Rows 1–3 on rem long edge of afghan.

Rep Row 1 only on both short edges of afghan.

Sailing, Sailing

Yellow sun, white sail, and red sailboat—they're captured in cross-stitch on a sea of brightest blue. Use cotton yarns for a summer throw as cool and crisp as a dash of sea spray.

FINISHED SIZE
Approximately 42″ square.

MATERIALS
Yarn description: Sportweight mercerized cotton.
Yarn pictured: Laines Anny Blatt Hawaii, Art. 21297, 50-gr. balls, 24 Gentiane #2694 (blue), 8 Blanc #2686 (white), 4 each Rouge #2595 (red), Genet #2696 (yellow).

TOOLS AND EQUIPMENT
Size G afghan hook, or size to obtain gauge; size G crochet hook; tapestry needle.

GAUGE
5 sts = 1″, 5 rows = 1″

DIRECTIONS
Afghan st: Row 1: *Step 1:* Keeping all lps on hook, draw up a lp through top lp only, in 2nd ch from hook and each ch across = same number of lps as chs. Do not turn.

Step 2: Yo and draw through first lp on hook, * yo and through 2 lps on hook; rep from * across (1 lp rem on hook for the first lp of next row). Do not turn.

Row 2: *Step 1:* Keeping all lps on hook, draw up a lp from under 2nd vertical bar, * draw up a lp from under next vertical bar; rep from * across. Do not turn.

Step 2: Rep Step 2 of Row 1.
Rep both steps of Row 2 for number of afghan st rows specified.

Block (make 16): With afghan hook and blue, ch 47. Work even in afghan st until 47 rows from the beg.

Row 48: Sl st in each vertical bar across. Fasten off.

Cross-stitch: Following chart and color key, work cross-stitch design on each block.

Border: Rnd 1: With crochet hook, join white in corner of block, * work 3 sc in corner, sc evenly to next corner; rep from * around block, join with sl st to first sc.

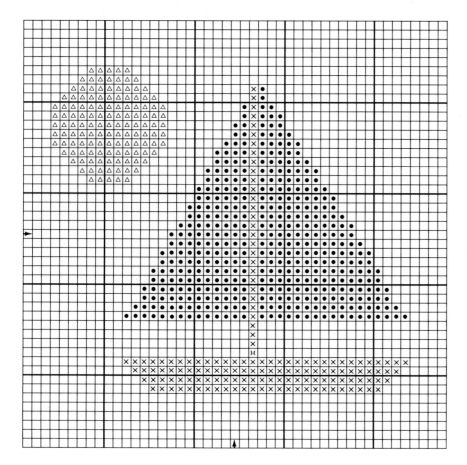

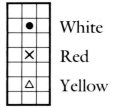

●	White
✕	Red
△	Yellow

Rnd 2: Sc in each sc around, work 3 sc in each corner. Join with sl st to first sc. Fasten off.

Rep Rnds 1 and 2 on each cross-stitched block.

Assembly: Arrange blocks in a 4-block x 4-block square. With right sides up, whipstitch blocks tog through back lps only, with white yarn.

Edging: Rnd 1: With crochet hook, join blue in any corner of afghan, work * 3 sc in corner, sc evenly to next corner; rep from * around, join with sl st to first sc.

Rnd 2: Sc in each sc around, work 3 sc in each corner. Join with sl st to first sc. Fasten off.

Blueberries 'n Cream

FINISHED SIZE
Approximately 42" square, not including fringe.

MATERIALS
Yarn description: Worsted-weight acrylic.
Yarn pictured: Reynolds Deluxe Reynelle®, 3½-oz. skeins, 5 Medium Blue #8014, 4 Cream #8079, 1 each Dark Blue #8013, Light Blue #8016, Dark Green #8024, Light Green #8025, Black #8061.

TOOLS AND EQUIPMENT
Size I afghan hook, or size to obtain gauge; size H crochet hook; tapestry needle.

GAUGE
4 sts = 1", 4 rows = 1"
Square = 8", including border

DIRECTIONS
Note: When working the chart in afghan st, work across row, drawing up lps in color indicated; work lps off by using same color as lp on hook. To avoid holes, bring up new color from under dropped color. Changing colors will be easier if yarn is wound on bobbins. If a color is to be used again in 4 sts or less, work over it with the next few sts and pick it up when needed. If a color is not needed for more than 4 sts, drop it to the wrong side of work and pick up when needed. Fasten off each color when no longer needed.

Afghan st: Row 1: *Step 1:* Keeping all lps on hook, draw up a lp through top lp only, in 2nd ch from hook and each ch across = same number of lps as chs. Do not turn.
Step 2: Yo and draw through first lp on hook, * yo and through 2 lps on hook; rep from * across (1 lp rem on hook for the first lp of next row). Do not turn.
Row 2: *Step 1:* Keeping all lps on hook, draw up a lp from under 2nd vertical bar, * draw up a lp from under next vertical bar; rep from * across. Do not turn.
Step 2: Rep Step 2 of Row 1.
Rep both steps of Row 2 for number of afghan st rows specified.
Note: Both steps of afghan st (see Row 2 above) equal 1 row on the chart. Read chart right to left for Step 1 and left to right for Step 2.

Square A (make 12): With afghan hook and cream, ch 24. Work even in afghan st until 24 rows from beg.
Row 25: Sl st in each vertical bar across. Fasten off.
Border: Rnd 1: With crochet hook, join medium blue in any corner, * work 3 sc in corner, work 23 sc evenly spaced to next corner; rep from * around as established. Join with sl st to first sc.
Rnds 2 and 3: Sc in each sc around, work 3 sc in each corner. Join with sl st to first sc. At end of Rnd 3, fasten off.
Rnd 4: Join cream in any corner and rep Rnd 2. Fasten off.

Summer afternoons shared with a friend—daydreams and laughter under the shade trees. Our blueberry afghan is a good summer friend, too, always ready for happy outings.

Row 17

Crochet Chart

Row 7

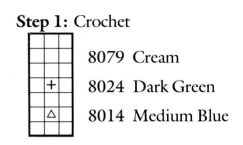

Step 1: Crochet

8079 Cream

+ 8024 Dark Green

△ 8014 Medium Blue

Cross-stitch Chart

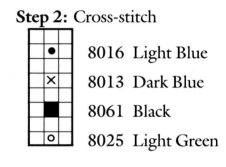

Step 2: Cross-stitch

● 8016 Light Blue

× 8013 Dark Blue

■ 8061 Black

○ 8025 Light Green

Square B (make 13): With afghan hook and cream, ch 24. Work even in afghan st for 6 rows.

Rows 7–17: Follow crochet chart and color key to work the blueberry design in afghan st.

Rows 18–24: Work even in cream and afghan st.

Row 25: Sl st in each vertical bar across. Fasten off.

Border: Work same as square A.

Cross-stitch: Work the cross-stitch highlights and shading on the blueberry design according to cross-stitch chart and color key.

Assembly: Beg with square B in corner, arrange squares in a 5-square x 5-square checkerboard pat. With right sides up and cream, whipstitch squares tog through front lps only.

Edging: Rnd 1: With crochet hook, join cream in any corner, * work 3 sc in corner, sc in each sc to next corner; rep from * around. Join with sl st to first sc.

Rnd 2: Sc in each sc around, work 3 sc in each corner. Fasten off.

Rnds 3–5: Join medium blue and rep Rnd 2.

Rnd 6: Ch 1, work 2 sc in corner, sc in next sc, * ch 2, sk 2 sc, sc in next 8 sc; rep from * to next corner, end with ch 2, sk 2 sc, 3 sc in corner, sc in next sc. Rep from * around as established. Join with sl st to first sc. Fasten off.

Fringe: Cut 10 (12") strands medium blue for each tassel. Knot a tassel through each ch-2 sp around afghan. Trim fringe even.

Over the Rainbow

FINISHED SIZE
Approximately 72″ x 84″.

MATERIALS
Yarn description: Sportweight mohair blend.
Yarn pictured: (No longer available; see suggested substitute below.) Pingouin Laine et Mohair, 130-yd. balls, 1 each of Bleu Roy #02 (color A), Floride #03 (B), Turquoise #04 (C), Evêque #05 (D), Fuchsia #06 (E), Rose Indien #07 (F), Gitane #08 (G), Soleil #09 (H), Angélique #10 (I), Persan #11 (J).
Substitute: Pingouin Mohair 50, Haiphong #545, Cobalt #529, Bleu Chinois #559, Lie de Vin #578, Brique #573, Fuchsia #558, Feu #531, Soleil #571, Véronèse #569, Cyprès #575.

TOOLS AND EQUIPMENT
Size N crochet hook, or size to obtain gauge.

GAUGE
4 sc = 3″

DIRECTIONS
With A, ch 119.

　　Row 1: Sc in 2nd ch from hook and in each ch across = 118 sc. Ch 1 and turn.

　　Row 2: Sc in each sc across. Ch 1 and turn.

　　Rep Row 2 with all of color A. Join B with final yo of last st in A, ch 1, and rep Row 2 with all of B. Continue in pat as established with rem colors.

Note: Change colors only at the end of a row. If the ball runs out in the middle of a row, pull out sts back to the beg of the row.

Simple stripes of single crochet make a shimmering rainbow.

Zinnia Garden

Bring in the sunshine and vibrant colors of midsummer with this lighthearted floral design. Make dimensional blossoms and appliqué them to a background of garden green.

FINISHED SIZE
Approximately 46" x 48".

MATERIALS
Yarn description: Worsted-weight acrylic.
Yarn pictured: Brunswick® Windrush Orlon®, 3½-oz. skeins, 7 Christmas Green #9043, 1 each Hot Pink #90081, Saffron Yellow #9008, Burnt Orange #90611, Flame Red #9026, White #9010, Purple #9014.

TOOLS AND EQUIPMENT
Size G crochet hook, or size to obtain gauge.

GAUGE
7 sts = 2"

DIRECTIONS
Afghan: With green, ch 158.
Row 1: Sc in 2nd ch from hook, * ch 1, sk 1 ch, sc in next ch; rep from * across, end with sc in last ch = 157 sc including starting ch. Ch 1, turn.
Row 2: Sc in first sc, * sc in ch-1 sp, ch 1; rep from * across, end with sc in last ch-1 sp, sc in last sc. Ch 1, turn.
Row 3: Sc in first sc, * ch 1, sc in next ch-1 sp; rep from * across, end with ch 1, sc in last sc. Ch 1, turn.
Rep Rows 2 and 3 until 45" from beg. At end of last row, fasten off.

Edging: Rnd 1: With green, sc evenly around entire afghan, working 3 sc in each corner. At end of rnd, join with sl st to first sc. Fasten off.

Rnd 2: With pink, ch 3 for first dc, dc in each sc around, working 3 dc in each corner. At end of rnd, join with sl st to top of starting ch. Fasten off.

Rnd 3: With purple, sc in each dc around, working 3 sc in each corner. At end of rnd, join with sl st to first sc. Fasten off.

Rnd 4: Join white 2 sts after center of any corner, sc in same st as joining, * dc in next st, tr in each of next 2 sts, dc in next st, sc in each of next 2 sts *; rep from * to * to next corner adjusting as necessary to have dc just before corner, work 6 tr in corner; rep from * to * to next corner. Continue around afghan as established; at end of rnd, join with sl st to first sc. Fasten off.

Zinnias: Make several zinnias in each color of yarn. (The center of each zinnia is red and yellow.)

Large zinnia: With red, ch 4, join with sl st to form a ring.

Rnd 1: Work 12 sc in ring, join with sl st to first sc. Fasten off.

Rnd 2: Join yellow, working in front lps only, sc in same st as joining, ch 2, sl st in 2nd ch from hook, sl st in same sc as joining, sl st in next sc, * sc in next sc, ch 2, sl st in 2nd ch from hook, sl st in same sc as last sl st, sl st in next sc; rep from * around, join with sl st to first sc. Fasten off.

Rnd 3: Join color for petals to back lp of sc on Rnd 1, working in back lps of Rnd 1 only, * sc and dc in next st, 2 tr in next st, dc and sc in next lp; rep from * around, join with sl st to first sc.

Rnd 4: * Ch 4, sk 1 petal, sl st between next 2 sc; rep from * around, end with ch 4, join with sl st to first ch of ch-4.

Rnd 5: * In next ch-4 work sc, dc, 2 tr, dc, and sc; rep from * around, join with sl st to first sc.

Rnd 6: * Ch 6, sk 1 petal, sl st between next 2 sc; rep from * around, end with ch 6, join with sl st to first ch of ch-6.

Rnd 7: * In next ch-6 work sc, 2 dc, 2 tr, 2 dc, and sc; rep from * around, join with sl st to first sc and fasten off.

Small zinnia: Follow instructions for large zinnia Rnds 1–5.

Finishing: Tack zinnias to afghan as desired (see photograph).

Rainbow Sampler

Show off your favorite crochet stitches—and learn new ones—in this summer-white, summer-bright design. Squares of many patterns—including shell, loop, arrow, and bobble—are bordered with rainbow stripes.

FINISHED SIZE
Approximately 54" x 66".

MATERIALS
Yarn description: Worsted-weight acrylic.
Yarn pictured: (No longer available; see suggested substitute below.) Coats & Clark Red Heart® Fabulend, Art. E.235, 45½ oz. Eggshell #111, 3½ oz. each Apricot #332, Apple Green #648, Devil Red #903, Lilac #586, Pink #737, Lemon #226.
Substitute: Coats & Clark Red Heart® 4-Ply Handknitting Yarn, Art. E.267, Eggshell #111, Orange #245, Mint Julep #669, Jockey Red #902, Lavender #584, Pink #737, Yellow #230.

TOOLS AND EQUIPMENT
Sizes I and J crochet hooks, or sizes to obtain measurements given.

DIRECTIONS

Shell st square (make 8): With larger hook and eggshell, ch 28 to measure 7¾".

Row 1 (right side): Work 2 dc in 4th ch from hook, * sk next 2 ch, sc in next ch, sk next 2 ch, 5 dc in next ch; rep from * to last 6 ch, end by sk next 2 ch, sc in next ch, sk next 2 ch, 3 dc in last ch. Ch 1, turn.

Row 2: Sc in first dc, * ch 2, sc in next sc, ch 2, sk next 2 dc, sc in next dc; rep from * across, end with sc in top of starting ch. Ch 1, turn.

Row 3: Sc in first sc, * 5 dc in next sc, sc in next sc; rep from * across. Ch 1, turn.

Row 4: Sc in first sc, * ch 2, sk next 2 dc, sc in next dc, ch 2, sc in next sc; rep from * across. Ch 3, turn.

Row 5: Work 2 dc in first sc, * sc in next sc, 5 dc in next sc; rep from * twice more, end with sc in next sc, 3 dc in last sc. Ch 1, turn.

Rep Rows 2–5 three times more, then rep Row 2 once more. Do not ch 1 at end of last row. Do not turn.

Border: With wrong side facing and smaller hook, ch 1, work * 3 sc in corner, sc evenly to next corner, rep from * around as established. Join with sl st to first sc. Fasten off.

Crossed-dc square (make 8): With smaller hook and eggshell, loosely ch 25 to measure 7½".

Row 1 (right side): Dc in 5th ch from hook, dc in 4th ch from hook, * sk next ch, dc in next ch, dc in sk ch; rep from * across = 23 sts including starting ch. Ch 3, turn.

Row 2: Sk first 2 dc, dc in next dc, dc in 2nd sk dc, * sk next dc, dc in next dc, dc in sk dc; rep from * to last dc and starting ch-3, end by sk last dc, dc in top of starting ch-3, dc in sk dc. Ch 3, turn.

Rep Row 2 eleven times more. Do not ch 3 at end of last row. Turn.

Work border as before.

Nubby st square (make 8): With smaller hook and eggshell, loosely ch 23 to measure 7¼".

Row 1 (right side): Sc and dc in 2nd ch from hook, * sk next ch, sc and dc in next ch; rep from * to last 3 ch, sk next ch, sc in next ch; keeping last 2 lps of each dc on hook, dc in same ch as previous sc, dc in last ch, yo and draw through all lps on hook (end st completed). Ch 1, turn.

Row 2: Sc and dc in end st, * sk next sc, sc and dc in next dc; rep from * to last 3 sts, sk next sc, sc in next dc, end st in previous sc and next sc. Ch 1 and turn.

Rep Row 2 until 7" from beg, end with right-side row. Do not ch 1 at end of last row. Turn.

Work border as before.

Lp st square (make 8): With smaller hook and eggshell, loosely ch 23 to measure 7¼".

Row 1 (right side): Sc in 2nd ch from hook and in each ch across = 22 sc. Ch 1, turn.

Row 2: Sc in first sc; * lp yarn over index finger of left hand from front to back, insert hook in next sc, pick up lp under finger, draw through, complete as a sc (lp st completed); rep from * across. Ch 1, turn.

Row 3: Sc in each st across. Ch 1 and turn.

Rep Rows 2 and 3 until 7" from beg, end with a wrong-side row. Do not ch 1 at the end of the last row. Do not turn.

Work border as before.

Arrow st square (make 8): With larger hook and eggshell, ch 25 to measure 7¼".

Row 1 (right side): Sc in 2nd ch from hook and in each ch across = 24 sc. Ch 1, turn.

Row 2: Sc in each sc across. Ch 3 and turn.

Row 3: Dc in next sc, * sk next 3

sc, yo and draw up a lp in next sc, yo and complete as a dc; holding dc to front of work, dc in each of the 3 sk sc; rep from * across to last 2 sts, end with dc in each of last 2 sts. Ch 3, turn.

Row 4: Dc in next dc, * sk next 3 dc, yo and draw up a lp in next dc, yo and complete as a dc; holding dc to back of work, dc in each of the 3 sk dc; rep from * across to last dc and turning ch, end with dc in next dc, dc in top of turning ch. Ch 1, turn.

Row 5: Sc in each st across. Ch 1 and turn.

Rep Rows 2–5 three times more. Do not ch 1 at end of last row. Turn.

Work border as before.

Bobble st square (make 8): With smaller hook and eggshell, loosely ch 24 to measure 7¼".

Row 1 (right side): Sc in 2nd ch from hook and in each ch across = 23 sc. Ch 1, turn.

Row 2: Sc in first sc, * tr in next sc, push tr to back of work to form bobble and sc in next sc; rep from * across. Ch 1, turn.

Row 3: Sc in each st across. Ch 1 and turn.

Row 4: Sc in first 2 sc, * tr in next sc, push tr to back of work to form bobble and sc in next sc; rep from * across to last sc, sc in last sc. Ch 1 and turn.

Row 5: Rep Row 3. Ch 1, turn.

Rep Rows 2–5 until 7" from beg, end with a right-side row. Do not ch 1 at end of last row. Turn.

Work border as before.

Strip assembly: Block all pieces to 7½" square. Arrange squares in 6 strips of 8 squares each. With smaller hook and wrong sides facing, sc squares tog through inner lps only. Join each succeeding square with a different color (except eggshell) until all colors have been used. For each strip use the colors in a different order.

Strip edging: Row 1: With smaller hook, join yarn to corner and ch 1, sc in corner, sc in each st across edge to next corner. Ch 1, turn.

Row 2: Sc in each sc across edge. Fasten off.

1st strip: With right sides facing and strip turned to work across right-hand edge, join lemon and work Rows 1 and 2. Do not work edging on left-hand edge.

2nd strip: Join lemon and work Rows 1 and 2 on left edge of strip. Rep Rows 1 and 2 on the right edge with lilac.

3rd strip: Work left edging with lilac, right edging with apricot.

4th strip: Work left edging with apricot, right edging with green.

5th strip: Work left edging with green, right edging with red.

6th strip: Work left edging with red. Do not work right edging.

Final assembly: With wrong sides facing, sc strips tog through inner lps only. Join strips 1 and 2 with red; 2 and 3 with pink; 3 and 4 with lemon; 4 and 5 with lilac; 5 and 6 with lemon.

Edging: Rnd 1: With right side of afghan facing and smaller hook, join apricot in any corner and ch 1, * 3 sc in corner, sc in each sc to next corner; rep from * around afghan. Join with sl st to first sc. Fasten off.

Rnds 2–6: Rep Rnd 1 with each of the following colors: green, pink, lilac, lemon, and red.

Firecracker

FINISHED SIZE
Approximately 56" x 77".

MATERIALS
Yarn description: Sportweight acrylic blend.

Yarn pictured: (Some colors no longer available; see substitutes.) Bernat® Berella® Sportspun, 2-oz. skeins, 6 Wedgwood, 5 Natural, 4 each Black, Baby Pink, 3 each Cranberry, Old Gold, Scarlet, 2 each Medium Orange, Yellow, Shannon Green.

Substitutes: For Medium Orange, use Summer Sunset; for Old Gold, Light Yellow.

TOOLS AND EQUIPMENT
Size F crochet hook, or size to obtain gauge; tapestry needle.

GAUGE
Square = 7"

DIRECTIONS
Square A (make 22): With natural, make a sl knot 3" from yarn end. Ch 6, join with sl st to form ring.

Rnd 1: Ch 3 for first dc, work 11 dc in ring (work sts over 3" end to conceal), join with sl st to top of starting ch = 12 dc including starting ch. Pull the 3" end to draw center sts tog.

Rnd 2: Ch 1, * in same dc work sc, ch 2, and sc (corner completed), sc in each of next 2 dc; rep from * 3 times more, join with sl st to first sc.

Rnd 3: Ch 1, sc in next sc, * in ch-2 corner work sc, ch 2, and sc (corner completed), sc in 4 sc; rep from * twice more, end with sc in last 3 sc, join with sl st to first sc.

Rnds 4 and 5: Ch 1, sc in each sc to corner, * work corner as before, sc in each sc to next corner; rep from * twice more, sc across last edge, join with sl st to first sc = 10 sc between ch-2 on each edge. At end of Rnd 5, fasten off.

Rnd 6: Join orange in any ch-2 corner, ch 1, * work corner in ch-2, sc in next sc, in next sc draw up a lp from st 1 row below, complete as sc (long sc completed), long sc in next st 2 rows below, long sc in next st 3 rows below, long sc in each of next 2 sts 4 rows below (center), long sc in next st 3 rows below, long sc in next st 2 rows below, long sc in next st 1 row below, sc in last sc before corner; rep from * 3 times more, join with sl st to first sc = 12 sts between ch-2 on each edge.

Rnd 7: Ch 1, sc in same sc as sl st, * work corner, sc in each of next 12 sc; rep from * 3 times more, join with sl st to first sc.

Rnds 8 and 9: Ch 1, sc to corner, * work corner, sc in each sc to next corner; rep from * 3 times more, join with sl st to first sc. At end of Rnd 9, fasten off.

Rnd 10: Join cranberry in any ch-2 corner, ch 1, * work corner, sc in next sc, long sc in next st 1 row below, long sc in next st 2 rows below, long sc in next st 3 rows below, long sc in next st 2 rows below, long sc in next st 1 row below, long sc in next st 2 rows below, long sc in each of next 2 sts 3 rows below (center), long sc in next st 2 rows below, long sc in next st 1 row below, long sc in next st 2 rows below, long sc in next st 3 rows below, long sc in next st 2 rows below, long sc in next st 1 row below, sc in sc before corner; rep from * 3 times more, join with sl st to first sc = 18 sts between ch-2 on each edge.

Put some excitement into your summer needlework with this razzle-dazzle design. Festive colors explode in a pattern that's bursting with snap, crack, and sizzle.

A	B	C	D	A	B	C	D
B	C	D	A	B	C	D	A
C	D	A	B	C	D	A	B
D	A	B	C	D	A	B	C
A	B	C	D	A	B	C	D
B	C	D	A	B	C	D	A
C	D	A	B	C	D	A	B
D	A	B	C	D	A	B	C
A	B	C	D	A	B	C	D
B	C	D	A	B	C	D	A
C	D	A	B	C	D	A	B

Rnds 11–13: Ch 1, sc to corner, * work corner in ch-1, sc evenly to next corner; rep from * 3 times more, join with sl st to first sc. After Rnd 13 = 24 sts between ch-2 on each edge. At end of Rnd 13, fasten off.

Rnd 14: Join gold in any ch-2 corner, ch 1, * work corner, sc in next sc, long sc in next st 1 row below, long sc in next st 2 rows below, long sc in next st 3 rows below, long sc in next st 2 rows below, long sc in each of next 3 sts 1 row below, long sc in next st 2 rows below, long sc in each of next 5 sts 3 rows below (center), long sc in next st 2 rows below, long sc in each of next 3 sts 1 row below, long sc in next st 2 rows below, long sc in next st 3 rows below, long sc in next st 2 rows below, long sc in next st 1 row below; rep from * 3 times more, join with sl st to first sc = 25 sts between ch-2 on each edge.

Rnd 15: Ch 1, sc evenly to corner, * work corner, sc evenly to next corner; rep from * 3 times more, join with sl st to first sc = 27 sts between ch-2 on each edge. Fasten off.

Rnd 16: Join black in ch-2 corner, ch 1, * work corner, sc evenly to next corner; rep from * 3 times more, join with sl st to first sc. Fasten off.

Square B (make 22): Work same as square A with the following color arrangement. Rnds 1–5: Scarlet. Rnds 6–9: Wedgwood. Rnds 10–13: Pink. Rnds 14 and 15: Natural. Rnd 16: Black.

Square C (make 22): Work the same as square A with the following color arrangement. Rnds 1–5: Pink. Rnds 6–9: Yellow. Rnds 10–13: Wedgwood. Rnds 14 and 15: Green. Rnd 16: Black.

Square D (make 22): Work same as square A with the following color arrangement. Rnds 1–5: Gold. Rnds 6–9: Scarlet. Rnds 10–13: Natural. Rnds 14 and 15: Wedgwood. Rnd 16: Black.

Assembly: Block all pieces to 7″ square. Using black and following diagram for placement, sew squares tog.

Edging: Rnd 1: Join black in any corner, ch 1, * work 3 sc in corner, sc evenly to next corner; rep from * 3 times more, join with sl st to first sc.

Rnd 2: Ch 1, sc in each sc around, work 3 sc in each corner. Join with sl st to first sc. Fasten off.

Pennsylvania Dutch

FINISHED SIZE
Afghan: approximately 48″ x 64″.
Pillow: approximately 14″ square.

MATERIALS
Yarn description: Worsted-weight acrylic.
Yarn pictured: (Some colors are no longer available; see suggested substitutes below.) Caron® Wintuk (a DuPont certification mark), 3½-oz. skeins, 12 White, 6 Royal (color A), 2 Devil Red (B), 1 each Leaf (C), Sunstream (D), a few yd. Black (E).
Substitutes: For Sunstream, use Yellow; for Leaf, New Leaf.
Other: 14″ pillow form.

The folk art designs on this colorful afghan decorate the barns of the Pennsylvania Dutch. These designs are said to bring good luck—and happy stitching!

TOOLS AND EQUIPMENT
Size J crochet hook, or size to obtain gauge; white tissue paper; tapestry needle.

GAUGE
17 sc = 5″
Square = 16″, including border

DIRECTIONS
Afghan: Square (make 12): With white, ch 49.

Row 1: Sc in 2nd ch from hook and in each ch across = 48 sc. Ch 1 and turn.

Row 2: Sc in each sc across. Ch 1 and turn.

Rep Row 2 until 14″ from beg. Fasten off.

Border: Rnd 1: Join white in any corner, ch 1, * work 3 sc in corner, sc evenly to next corner; rep from * around square, join with sl st to first sc. Fasten off.

Rnd 2: Join B in any corner and sc evenly around square, work 3 sc in each corner. Fasten off.

Rnds 3 and 4: Join A in any corner and rep Rnd 2 twice. At end of Rnd 4, fasten off.

Embroidery: Enlarge embroidery patterns and transfer to 16″ squares of tissue paper (see placement diagram for how many of each motif to make). Center patterns on crocheted squares. Baste paper patterns to squares and embroider designs through paper. (*Note:* Broken line on flower cluster design is for placement only; do not embroider.) Use satin stitch for leaves and flowers; stem stitch for stems; backstitch for bird; chain stitch for circles on hex sign and bird designs; French knots for small circles of color C. When embroidery is completed, tear paper patterns away from squares and tease from under embroidery.

Assembly: Referring to placement diagram, use A to sew squares tog through the back lps only.

Edging: Rnds 1 and 2: Join A in any corner, * work 3 sc in corner, sc evenly to next corner; rep from * around afghan, join with sl st to first sc. At end of Rnd 2, fasten off.

Pillow: Make 2 squares as for afghan. Embroider bird design on one square. With wrong sides facing, use A to sew pieces tog around 3 sides. Insert pillow form and sew rem side closed.

Edging: Rnd 1: Join A in corner and, working through both thicknesses, sc evenly around pillow, work 3 sc in each corner. Join with sl st to first sc.

Rnds 2–4: Sc evenly around pillow, work 3 sc in each corner, join with sl st to first sc. At end of Rnd 4, fasten off.

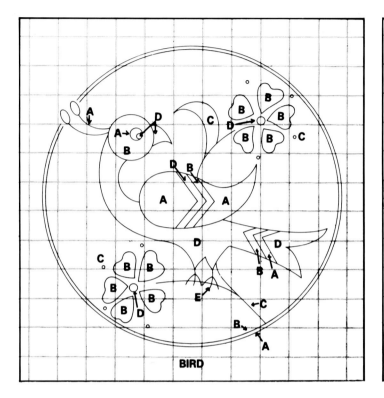

BIRD

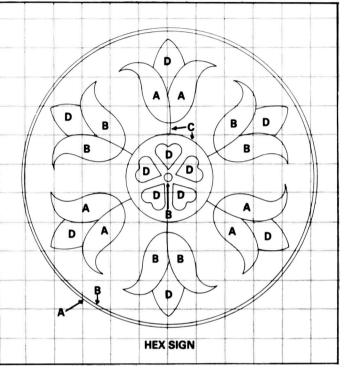

HEX SIGN

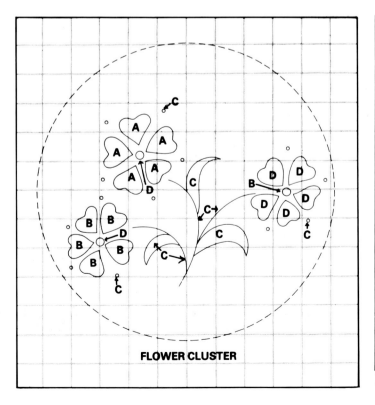

FLOWER CLUSTER

HEX SIGN	FLOWER	HEX SIGN
FLOWER	BIRD	REVERSE FLOWER
FLOWER	REVERSE BIRD	REVERSE FLOWER
HEX SIGN	REVERSE FLOWER	HEX SIGN

Placement Diagram

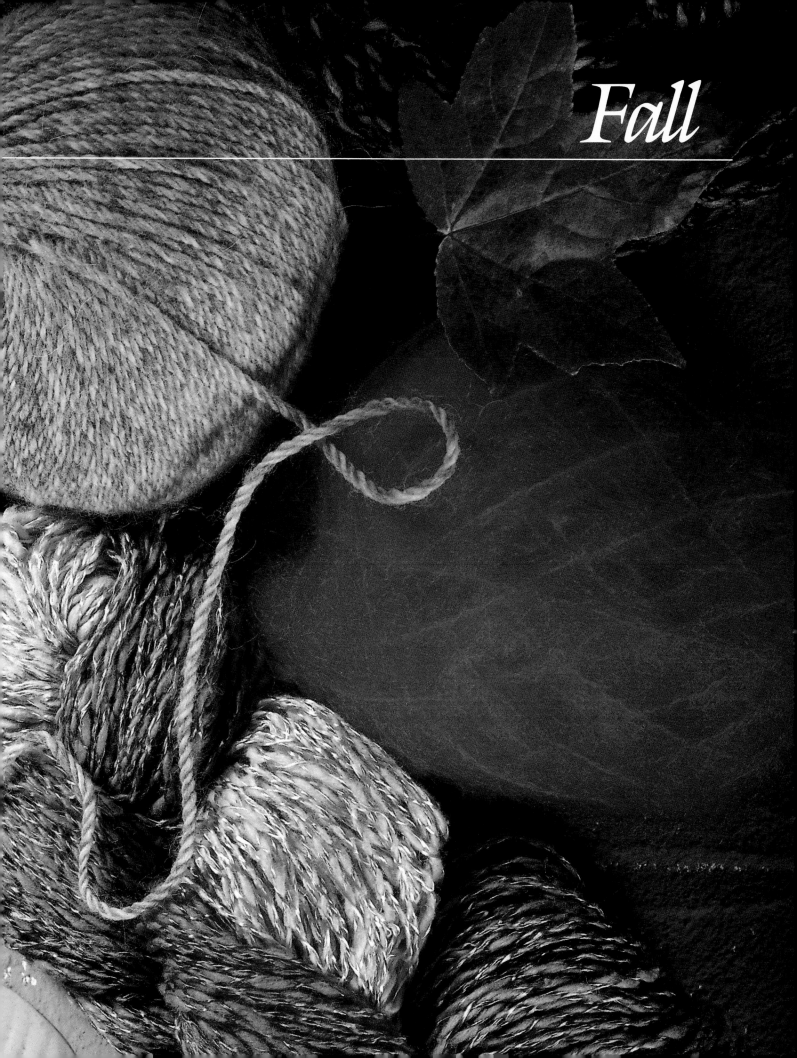

Fall

Indian Blanket

Indian summer calls for a throw touched with turquoise, sand, and gold. Make the panels as directed, and ornament them with stitchery inspired by native American designs.

FINISHED SIZE
Approximately 50″ x 70″.

MATERIALS
Yarn description: Worsted-weight machine-washable wool.
Yarn pictured: Scheepjeswol® Superwash Plus, 50-gr. skeins, 22 Cream #7626, 10 Neutral #7653, 6 each Yellow #7658, Brick #7603, Brown #7655, Jade #7654.

TOOLS AND EQUIPMENT
Size J afghan hook, size I crochet hook, or sizes to obtain gauge; tapestry needle.

GAUGE
4 hdc = 1″, 3 rows = 1″

DIRECTIONS
Afghan st: Row 1: *Step 1:* Keeping all lps on hook, draw up a lp through top lp only, in 2nd ch from hook and each ch across = same number of lps as chs. Do not turn.

Step 2: Yo and draw through first lp on hook, * yo and through 2 lps on hook; rep from * across (1 lp rem on hook for the first lp of next row). Do not turn.

Row 2: *Step 1:* Keeping all lps on hook, draw up a lp from under 2nd vertical bar, * draw up a lp from under next vertical bar; rep from * across. Do not turn.

Step 2: Rep Step 2 of Row 1.
Rep both steps of Row 2 for number of afghan st rows specified.

Cross-stitch panels (make 2): With afghan hook and cream, ch 37. Work in afghan st until 200 rows from beg.

Row 201: Sc across row by inserting hook under each vertical bar. Fasten off.

Block each panel. Beg at left-hand edge of panel, work cross-stitch design to center point according to chart and color key. Reverse design at center for mirror image.

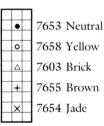

●	7653 Neutral
○	7658 Yellow
△	7603 Brick
+	7655 Brown
✕	7654 Jade

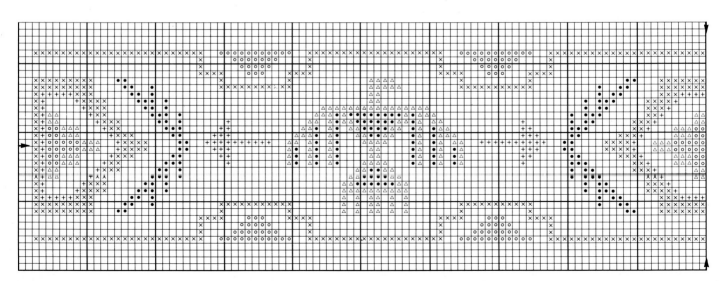

Center panels: Row 1: Using crochet hook, with cross-stitched panel turned to work across top edge and right side facing, join brick in corner, ch 2 for first hdc, * hdc in each of next 2 sts (row edges), yo and draw up a lp from 2 rows below, complete as a dc (long dc completed); rep from * across, end with hdc in each of last 3 sts. Turn.

Row 2: Ch 2 for first hdc, hdc in each st across. Fasten off. Turn.

Rows 3–12: Join yellow and rep Row 2. At end of Row 12, fasten off.

Row 13: Join jade and rep Row 1.

Rows 14–16: Rep Row 2. At end of Row 16, fasten off.

Rows 17 and 18: Join brown; rep Row 2. At end of Row 18, fasten off.

Row 19: Join cream yarn and rep Row 1.

Rows 20–37: Rep Row 2. At end of Row 37, fasten off.

Row 38: Join brick; rep Row 1.

Rows 39–41: Rep Row 2. At end of Row 41, fasten off.

Row 42: Join neutral and rep Row 1.

Row 43: Rep Row 2. Fasten off.

Rows 44–47: Join cream and rep Row 2. At end of Row 47, fasten off.

Rows 48 and 49: Join brown; rep Row 2. At end of Row 49, fasten off.

Row 50: Join jade and rep Row 1.

Row 51: Rep Row 2. Fasten off.

Rows 52–59: Join neutral and rep Row 2. At end of Row 59, fasten off.

Rep Rows 1–59 on the rem cross-stitched panel.

Match Row 59 of each panel and whipstitch tog with neutral.

End panels: Row 1: Using crochet hook, with cross-stitched panel turned to work across bottom edge and right side facing, join brick in corner, ch 2 for first hdc, * hdc in each of next 2 sts (row edges), yo and draw up a lp from 2 rows below, complete as dc (long dc completed); rep from * across, end with hdc in each of last 3 sts. Turn.

Row 2: Ch 2 for first hdc, hdc in each st across. Fasten off. Turn.

Rows 3–6: Join brown; rep Row 2. At the end of Row 6, fasten off.

Row 7: Join cream; rep Row 1.

Rows 8–10: Rep Row 2. At the end of Row 10, fasten off.

Row 11: Join neutral and rep Row 1.

Rows 12–20: Rep Row 2. At the end of Row 20, fasten off.

Row 21: Join cream; rep Row 1.

Rows 22–28: Rep Row 2. At the end of Row 28, fasten off.

Rep Rows 1–28 on rem cross-stitched panel.

Edging: Rnd 1: With right side facing, join cream in any corner, work 3 sc in corner, * sc evenly to next corner, work 3 sc in corner; rep from * around afghan. Join with sl st to first sc.

Rnd 2: Rep Rnd 1. Fasten off.

Back to School Afghan

FINISHED SIZE
Approximately 48" x 57", not including fringe.

MATERIALS
Yarn description: Worsted-weight acrylic.

Yarn pictured: (No longer available; see suggested substitute below.) Columbia-Minerva® Nantuck®, 4-oz. balls, 3 each Gold (color A), Medium Avocado (B); Columbia-Minerva® Heathers and Ombres, 3-oz. balls, 3 Avocado (C).

Substitute: Columbia-Minerva® Windspun™ or Nantuck Brushed™ in colors of choice.

TOOLS AND EQUIPMENT
Size I crochet hook, or size to obtain gauge; tapestry needle.

GAUGE
3 mesh = 2"

DIRECTIONS
Mesh pat: Worked on an uneven number of sts.

   Row 1: Dc in 6th ch from hook, * ch 1, sk 1 ch, dc in next ch; rep from * across. Turn.

   Row 2: Ch 4 for first dc and ch 1, * dc in next dc, ch 1; rep from * across, end by sk 1 ch on starting ch, dc in next ch.

   Rep Row 2 for mesh pat.

Afghan: With color B, ch 164. Work in mesh pat in the following colors: * 1 more row color B, 4 rows A, 2 rows B, 4 rows C; rep from * 6 times more, end with 2 rows B. Fasten off.

Finishing: Cut yarn lengths 16" longer than the length of the afghan. Thread tapestry needle with 4 strands of yarn for each row of weaving. Weave from lower edge of afghan to top edge in vertical rows. *Note:* Weave strands through mesh fairly loosely so that the work will not be too taut. Beg at left side edge with * 2 rows B, 4 rows A, 2 rows B, 4 rows C; rep from * twice more; then weave 1 row each B, A, C, B, A, C, B; continue with ** 4 rows A, 2 rows B, 4 rows C, 2 rows B; rep from ** twice more (79 rows total). Trim fringe even.

To make this afghan, crochet a striped mesh—then weave it with strands of yarn. Stitch it in fall's greens and golds, or use school colors for a back-to-school present full of warm wishes.

Mossy Stones

Fly in your mind to a cool mountain retreat, touched by the sparkle and spray of a rushing stream. Mixed tones of blue and green, and an interesting loop-stitch edging, capture the play of light on mossy stones.

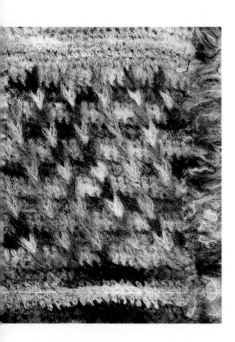

FINISHED SIZE
Approximately 45″ x 60″.

MATERIALS
Yarn description: Worsted-weight brushed wool blend and wool-blend bouclé.

Yarn pictured: (Some colors are no longer available; see suggested substitutes below.) Berroco, Inc. Dji Dji, brushed wool blend, 50-gr. skeins, 8 each Sky Mist #8523 (color A), Sea Mist #8451 (B); Berroco, Inc. Tiffany, wool-blend bouclé, 6 Aqua #5562 (C).

Substitutes: For Sea Mist #8451, use Peacock Mist #8437; for Aqua #5562, Horizon #5740.

TOOLS AND EQUIPMENT
Size J crochet hook, or size to obtain gauge.

GAUGE
4 sc = 1″
Square = 8″, including border

DIRECTIONS
Note: Always work with 2 strands of yarn held tog as one.

A and B striped square (make 16): With A, ch 24.

Row 1: Sc in 2nd ch from hook and in each sc across = 23 sc. Ch 1 and turn.

Row 2: Sc in each sc across. Fasten off. Turn.

Row 3 (right side): Join B, sc in each of next 3 sc, * yo and insert hook around post of sc 2 rows below, draw up a long lp, complete as a dc (post dc completed), sc in each of next 3 sc; rep from * across = 23 sts. Ch 1, turn.

Row 4: Sc in each st across. Fasten off. Turn.

Row 5: Join A, sc in 4 sc, * work post dc around post of st 2 rows below, sc in each of next 3 sc; rep from * across, end last rep with sc in each of 2 sc. Ch 1, turn.

Row 6: Sc in each st across. Fasten off. Turn.

Row 7: Join B, sc in next sc, * post dc around post of st 2 rows below, sc in 3 sc; rep from * across, end by omitting 2 sc at end of last rep. Ch 1 and turn.

Row 8: Sc in each st across. Fasten off. Turn.

Row 9: Join A, sc in 2 sc; * post dc around post of st 2 rows below, sc in 3 sc; rep from * across, end last rep with sc in each of last 4 sc. Ch 1, turn.

Rows 10–24: Rep Rows 2–9, ending with a sc row.

Border: Join C in any corner, work * 3 sc in corner, sc evenly to next corner; rep from * 3 times more, join with sl st to first sc. Fasten off.

A square (make 8): With A, work in same manner as A and B striped square (omit color changes). Work border same as before with C.

B square (make 5): With B, work in same manner as A and B striped square (omit color changes). Work border same as before with C.

C square (make 6): With C, work in same manner as A and B striped square (omit color changes). Work border same as before with C.

Strip assembly: With wrong sides facing, sc squares tog according to placement diagram, using C. Join squares into strips of 7 squares each.

Strip border: Row 1: With wrong side facing and strip turned to work across long edge, join color C and sc evenly across edge. Fasten off. Do not turn.

Row 2 (wrong side): With one strand each of colors A and B held tog as one, sc in first sc, * lp yarn over index finger of left hand from front to back, insert hook in st, pick up lp under finger, draw through, and complete as a sc (lp st completed); rep from * across, end with sc in last sc and fasten off.

Rep Rows 1 and 2 on the left edge of each strip of squares.

Final assembly: With right sides facing, sl st strips tog across long edges according to placement diagram. Be careful not to catch lp sts in seam.

Rep strip border Rows 1 and 2 on right edge of afghan.

Edging: Row 1: With right side facing, join color C in any corner and sc evenly to next corner. Ch 1, turn.

Row 2: Sc in each sc across and fasten off.

Rep Rows 1 and 2 for each rem edge of afghan.

C	C	A and B STRIPED	A	A and B STRIPED
C	A and B STRIPED	A	A and B STRIPED	B
A and B STRIPED	A	A and B STRIPED	B	A and B STRIPED
A	A and B STRIPED	B	A and B STRIPED	A
A and B STRIPED	B	A and B STRIPED	A	A and B STRIPED
B	A and B STRIPED	A	A and B STRIPED	C
A and B STRIPED	A	A and B STRIPED	C	C

Ripple Afghan

Work this traditional favorite in up-and-down waves of berry, lavender, grenadine, gray, and orchid bordered with black.

FINISHED SIZE
Approximately 51" x 79".

MATERIALS
Yarn description: Worsted-weight acrylic.

Yarn pictured: Coats & Clark Red Heart® 4-ply Handknitting Yarn, Art. E.267, 3½-oz. skeins, 8 Black #12, 1 each Berry #743, Lavender #584, Gray #404, Grenadine #730, Orchid #575.

TOOLS AND EQUIPMENT
Size F crochet hook, or size to obtain gauge.

GAUGE
9 sc = 2"

DIRECTIONS
With black, ch 270.

Row 1: Sc in 2nd ch from hook and in each of next 11 ch, * 3 sc in next ch, sc in each of next 12 ch, sk 2 ch, sc in each of next 12 ch; rep from * across to last 14 ch, end with 3 sc in next ch, sc in each of next 12 sts, sc in last ch. Ch 1, turn.

Row 2: Working in back lps only, sc in next sc, sk 1 sc, sc in each of next 10 sc, * 3 sc in next sc, sc in each of next 12 sc, sk 2 sc, sc in each of next 12 sc; rep from * across to last 14 sc, end with 3 sc in next sc, sc in each of 10 sc, sk 1 sc, sc in last sc. Ch 1, turn.

Rep Row 2 as follows: 9 more rows black, * 3 rows berry, 2 rows black, 3 rows lavender, 2 rows black, 3 rows gray, 2 rows black, 3 rows grenadine, 2 rows black, 3 rows orchid, 10 rows black; rep from * 5 times more. Fasten off.

Falling Leaves

Plum, gold, green, and brown: the colors of autumn meet and mingle in this cozy throw. Complement the lacy pattern of filet crochet leaves with a soft, multicolored fringe.

FINISHED SIZE
Approximately 53″ x 71″, not including fringe.

MATERIALS
Yarn description: Bulky-weight acrylic blend.
Yarn pictured: Neveda® Mondial, 100-gr. skeins, 3 each Green #7144, Gold #7120, Brown #7122, Berry #7127, Plum #7125.

TOOLS AND EQUIPMENT
Size G crochet hook, or size to obtain gauge; tapestry needle.

GAUGE
4 dc = 1″, 2 rows = 1″

DIRECTIONS
Block A (make 10 = 4 green, 3 berry, 2 gold, 1 plum): Ch 56.

Row 1: Dc in 8th ch from hook, * ch 2, sk 2 ch, dc in next ch; rep from * across = 17 mesh. Ch 5, turn (Row 1 of chart A completed).

Row 2: * Dc in next dc, ch 2; rep from * across, end by sk 2 chs on starting ch, dc in next ch. Ch 5, turn (Row 2 of chart A completed).

Row 3: Following Row 3 of chart A, [dc in next dc, ch 2] 7 times, dc in next dc, 2 dc in next ch-2 sp (filled mesh completed), [dc in next dc, ch 2] 8 times, dc in 3rd ch of turning ch. Ch 5, turn.

Rows 4–26: Follow chart A as established. At end of Row 26, do not turn or fasten off.

Border: Ch 3 for first dc, work 4 dc in same corner sp, * dc in each dc post and in each sp *; rep from * to * to next corner, 5 dc in corner; ** dc in next dc, 2 dc in next sp **; rep from ** to ** to next corner, 5 dc in corner; rep from * to * to next corner, 5 dc in corner; rep from ** to ** to next corner; sl st to top of ch-3. Fasten off.

Block B (make 10 = 4 brown, 3 plum, 2 gold, 1 berry): Ch 56.

Rows 1 and 2: Work same as block A, Rows 1 and 2.

Row 3: Following Row 3 of chart B, [dc in next dc, ch 2] 6 times, dc in next dc, 2 dc in next ch-2 sp (filled mesh completed), [dc in next dc, ch 2] 9 times, dc in 3rd ch of turning ch. Ch 5, turn.

Rows 4–26: Follow chart B as established. At end of Row 26, do not turn or fasten off.

Border: Work same as block A.

Assembly: With right sides up and referring to diagram for placement, whipstitch blocks tog.

Edging: Rnd 1: Join green in any corner, * 3 sc in corner, sc evenly to next corner; rep from * around, join with sl st to first sc.

Rnd 2: Sc to corner, * 3 sc in center sc of corner, sc in each sc to next corner; rep from * around, join with sl st to first sc. Fasten off.

Fringe: For each tassel, cut 1 (9″) strand of each color. Knot tassels about 1″ apart around entire afghan. Make a 2nd row of knots in fringe by knotting tog 5 strands from one tassel and 5 from the next tassel about 1″ below the first knot.

Row 26

Row 3

Row 2

Row 1

Chart A

Row 26

Row 3

Row 2

Row 1

Chart B

GREEN A	PLUM B	GOLD A	BERRY B
BROWN B	GREEN A	PLUM B	GOLD A
BERRY A	BROWN B	GREEN A	PLUM B
GOLD B	BERRY A	BROWN B	GREEN A
PLUM A	GOLD B	BERRY A	BROWN B

Placement Diagram

71

Game Birds

Rich fall tones worked in a variety of stitches form the sampler blocks for this crazy-quilt afghan. On the cream-colored squares, use favorite bits of scrapbag yarn to embroider ducks and dragonflies.

FINISHED SIZE
Approximately 45″ x 62″.

MATERIALS
Yarn description: Worsted-weight acrylic.

Yarn pictured: (Some colors are no longer available; see suggested substitutes below.) Brunswick® Windrush Orlon®, 100-gr. skeins, 3 Parchment #9030 (color 1), 2 each Brown #90341 (2), Caramel #9073 (3), Coffee #90292 (4), Earth Green #9085 (5), Meadow Green #9083 (6), Cardinal #9036 (7); several yd. each Powder Blue #9011, Gray Heather #90621, White #9010, Medium Gray Heather #90622, Dark Coffee #90293, Dark Gray Heather #90623, Gold #9005, Cranberry #90423, Black #9060, Honey #9027.

Substitutes: For Meadow Green #9083, use Dark Juniper #90573; for Gold #9005, Dark Goldenrod #90383; for Cranberry #90423, Dark Winterberry #90873; for Honey #9027, Goldenrod #90381.

TOOLS AND EQUIPMENT
Size H crochet hook, or size to obtain gauge; tapestry needle.

GAUGE
7 sts = 2″, 4 rows = 1″ (sc, ridge st, and pineapple st)
4 sts = 1″, 4 rows = 1″ (afghan st)

DIRECTIONS
Ridge st: Work a ch the required length.

Row 1: Sc in 2nd ch from hook and in each ch across. Ch 1, turn.

Row 2: Working in front lp only, sc in each sc across. Ch 1, turn.

Rep Row 2 for ridge st.

Sc: Work a ch the required length.

Row 1: Sc in 2nd ch from hook and in each ch across. Ch 1, turn.

Row 2: Sc in each sc across. Ch 1 and turn.

Rep Row 2 for sc.

Pineapple st: Work a ch the required length.

Row 1: Sc in 2nd ch from hook and in each ch across. Ch 1, turn.

Row 2: Sc in each of next 3 sts [yo and draw up a lp] 4 times in next st, yo and through 8 lps on hook, yo and through 2 lps on hook (pineapple st completed), * sc in each of next 5 sts, pineapple st in next sc; rep from * across, end with sc in last 3 sts. Ch 1 and turn.

Row 3: Sc in each sc and pineapple st across. Ch 1, turn.

Row 4: Sc in 6 sts, * pineapple st in next st, sc in each of next 5 sts; rep from * across, end with sc in last 6 sts.

Row 5: Sc in each sc and pineapple st across.

Rows 6–9: Rep Rows 2–5.

Rep Rows 2–9 for pineapple st.

Afghan st: Work a ch the required length.

Row 1: *Step 1:* Keeping all lps on hook, draw up a lp through top lp only, in 2nd ch from hook and each ch across = same number of lps as chs. Do not turn.

Step 2: Yo and draw through first lp on hook, * yo and through 2 lps on hook; rep from * across (1 lp rem on hook for the first lp of next row). Do not turn.

Row 2: *Step 1:* Keeping all lps on hook, draw up a lp from under 2nd vertical bar, * draw up a lp from under next vertical bar; rep from * across. Do not turn.

Step 2: Rep Step 2 of Row 1.

Rep both steps of Row 2 for number of afghan st rows specified.

Afghan: *Note:* In instructions below, the letter designates the block in the assembly diagram; the number indicates color.

Block A: With color 3, ch 36. Work in ridge st for 108 rows. Fasten off.

Block B: With color 2, ch 36. Work in sc for 12 rows. Fasten off.

Block C: With color 7, ch 36. Work in pineapple st for 24 rows. Fasten off.

Block D: With color 4, ch 47. Work in sc for 36 rows. Fasten off.

Block E: With color 1, ch 91. Work in afghan st for 64 rows. Fasten off.

Block F: With color 5, ch 43. Work in sc for 16 rows. Fasten off.

Block G: With color 6, ch 26. Work in sc for 24 rows. Fasten off.

Block H: With color 3, ch 61. Work in ridge st for 28 rows. Fasten off.

Block I: With color 2, ch 14. Work in sc for 68 rows. Fasten off.

Block J: With color 7, ch 19. Work in pineapple st for 24 rows. Fasten off.

Block K: With color 5, ch 15. Work in sc for 72 rows. Fasten off.

Block L: With color 6, ch 50. Work in sc for 24 rows. Fasten off.

Block M: With color 1, ch 54. Work in afghan st for 47 rows. Fasten off.

Block N: With color 7, ch 33. Work in pineapple st for 56 rows. Fasten off.

Block O: With color 5, ch 33. Work in sc for 16 rows. Fasten off.

Block P: With color 4, ch 64. Work in sc for 36 rows. Fasten off.

Block Q: With color 3, ch 40. Work in ridge st for 36 rows. Fasten off.

Block R: With color 6, ch 26. Work in sc for 36 rows. Fasten off.

Block S: With color 7, ch 29. Work in pineapple st for 24 rows. Fasten off.

Block T: With color 4, ch 50. Work in sc for 24 rows. Fasten off.

Block U: With color 3, ch 78. Work in ridge st for 44 rows. Fasten off.

Block V: With color 1, ch 40. Work in afghan st for 33 rows. Fasten off.

Block W: With color 5, ch 47. Work in sc for 12 rows. Fasten off.

Block X: With color 2, ch 47. Work in sc for 24 rows. Fasten off.

Block Y: With color 7, ch 26. Work in sc for 32 rows. Fasten off.

Block Z: With color 4, ch 56. Work in sc for 32 rows. Fasten off.

Cross-stitch: Block all pieces to measurements on placement diagram.

Work the cross-stitch designs according to charts and color key. On block E, work Wood Duck with Cattails; on block M, Green-Winged Teal with Dragonfly; on block V, Water Lily.

Assembly: With wrong sides facing and color 4, sc blocks tog according to placement diagram.

Edging: Rnd 1: Join color 4 in any corner with sl st, in same st work sc, ch 2, and sc, * sc evenly to next corner, in corner work sc, ch 2, and sc; rep from * around as established. Join with sl st to first sc.

Rnd 2: Ch 3 for first dc, dc in each sc around, in each ch-2 corner work dc, ch 2, and dc. At end of rnd, join with sl st to starting ch. Fasten off.

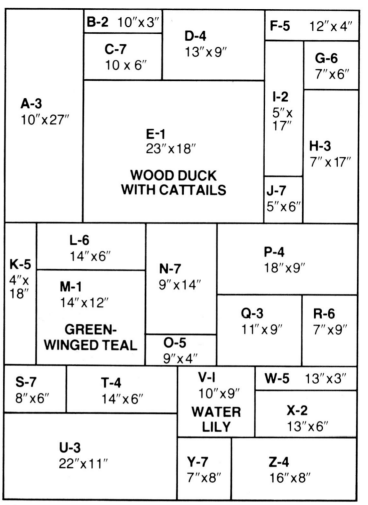

Placement Diagram

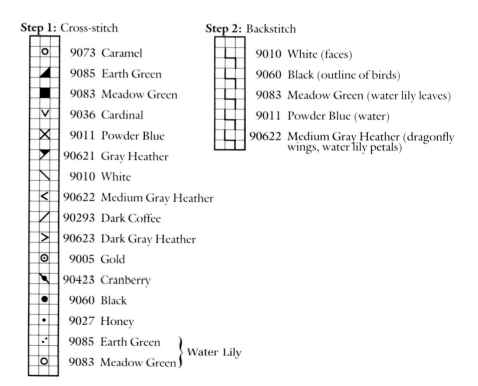

Step 1: Cross-stitch

◔	9073 Caramel
◤	9085 Earth Green
■	9083 Meadow Green
V	9036 Cardinal
X	9011 Powder Blue
▶	90621 Gray Heather
◣	9010 White
<	90622 Medium Gray Heather
/	90293 Dark Coffee
>	90623 Dark Gray Heather
◉	9005 Gold
◥	90423 Cranberry
●	9060 Black
⋅	9027 Honey
⦂	9085 Earth Green
◎	9083 Meadow Green	} Water Lily

Step 2: Backstitch

	9010 White (faces)
	9060 Black (outline of birds)
	9083 Meadow Green (water lily leaves)
	9011 Powder Blue (water)
	90622 Medium Gray Heather (dragonfly wings, water lily petals)

Wood Duck with Cattails

Green-Winged Teal with Dragonfly

Water Lily

75

Popcorn Afghan

Texture is the prize in this blue-ribbon winner, as full of fall fun as a county fair. Use playful popcorn stitches for rows of diamonds and finish with a picot edge.

FINISHED SIZE
Approximately 47" x 70".

MATERIALS
Yarn description: Worsted-weight acrylic.
Yarn pictured: (Color is no longer available; see suggested substitute below.) Caron® DazzleAire™, 3-oz. skeins, 15 Pumpkin.
Substitute: For Pumpkin, use Peach.

TOOLS AND EQUIPMENT
Size G crochet hook, or size to obtain gauge.

GAUGE
7 sts = 1"

DIRECTIONS
Note: Each row must have exactly 143 sts including ch 1 or ch 3, which count as the first st of each row. Each completed popcorn st counts as one st.

All right-side rows are dc and popcorn st; all wrong-side rows are sc.

Popcorn st: Work 5 dc in same st, draw up a long lp in last st and drop lp from hook, insert hook in first dc of 5-dc group, pick up dropped lp, draw through and tighten (1 popcorn st completed).

Afghan: Ch 144.
Row 1: Sc in 3rd ch from hook (ch before first sc counts as first st of row), sc in each ch across; ch 3, turn.

Row 2: Dc in 2nd sc, dc in next 9 sc, popcorn st in next sc, * dc in next 19 sc, popcorn st in next sc; rep from * 5 times more, dc in next 10 sc, dc in starting ch; ch 1, turn.

Row 3: Sc in 2nd dc, sc in each dc and in top of each popcorn st across row, sc in top ch of turning ch; ch 3 and turn.

Note: Immediately to the left of each popcorn st on the wrong side, there will appear to be a st. This is actually part of the popcorn st. Do not sc in this place or you will have extra sts in the row.

Row 4: Dc in 2nd sc, dc in next 7 sc, popcorn st in next sc, dc in next 3 sc, popcorn st in next sc, * dc in next 15 sc, popcorn st in next sc, dc in next 3 sc, popcorn st in next sc; rep from * 5 times more, dc in next 9 sc; ch 1 and turn.

Row 5: Rep Row 3.
Row 6: Dc in 2nd sc, dc in next 5 sc, * popcorn st in next sc, dc in next 7 sc, popcorn st in next sc, dc in next 11 sc; rep from * 5 times more, [popcorn st in next sc, dc in next 7 sc] twice; ch 1, turn.

Row 7: Rep Row 3.
Row 8: Dc in 2nd sc, dc in next 3 sc, * popcorn st in next sc, dc in next 11 sc, popcorn st in next sc, dc in next 7 sc; rep from * 5 times more, popcorn st in next sc, dc in next 11 sc, popcorn st in next sc, dc in next 5 sc; ch 1, turn.

Row 9: Rep Row 3.

Row 10: Dc in 2nd sc, dc in next sc, * popcorn st in next sc, dc in next 6 sc, popcorn st in next sc, dc in next sc, popcorn st in next sc, dc in next 6 sc, popcorn st in next sc, dc in next 3 sc, popcorn st in next sc, dc in next 15 sc, popcorn st in next sc, dc in next 3 sc; rep from * twice more, ** popcorn st in next sc, dc in next 6 sc, popcorn st in next sc **, dc in next sc; rep from ** to ** once, dc in next 3 sc; ch 1, turn.

Row 11: Rep Row 3.

Row 12: * Popcorn st in next sc, dc in next 6 sc, [popcorn st in next sc, dc in next 2 sc] twice, popcorn st in next sc, dc in next 6 sc, [popcorn st in next sc, dc in next 9 sc] twice; rep from * twice more, popcorn st in next sc, dc in next 6 sc, [popcorn st in next sc, dc in next 2 sc] twice, popcorn st in next sc, dc in next 6 sc, popcorn st in next sc, dc in next sc; ch 1, turn.

Odd Rows 13–21: Rep Row 3.

Row 14: Rep Row 10.

Row 16: Rep Row 8.

Row 18: Rep Row 6.

Row 20: Rep Row 4.

Row 22: Dc in 2nd sc, * dc in next 9 sc, popcorn st in next sc; rep from * 12 times more, dc in next 11 sc; ch 1 and turn.

Rows 23–142: Rep Rows 3–22, 6 times. (*Note:* To follow the pat more easily, write down the numbers 3–22 and cross off each number as you complete the row.)

Rows 143–161: Rep Rows 3–21.

Row 162: Rep Row 2.

Row 163: Rep Row 3. Ch 1 at end of row is first st of edge. (Do not fasten off.) Turn.

Edging: Rnd 1: With right side facing, sc evenly to the next corner, work 3 sc in corner; work 2 sc in each dc and 1 sc in each sc to next corner, work 3 sc in corner; sc evenly to next corner, work 3 sc in corner; work 2 sc in each dc and 1 sc in each sc to next corner, work 2 sc in corner; join with sl st to first sc.

Rnd 2: Ch 6, sl st in 4th ch from hook (picot completed), ch 1, * sk 1 sc, dc in next sc, ch 3, sl st in top of dc (picot), ch 1; rep from * to next corner; work dc, picot, ch 1 in each of 3 sc in corner (corner completed); sk 1 sc, continue around afghan as established. In last corner, [dc, picot, ch 1] twice, sl st in 3rd ch (just below picot) to join. Fasten off.

Folk Art Florals

FINISHED SIZE
Afghan: approximately 45″ x 60″.
Pillow: approximately 16″ square.

MATERIALS
Yarn description: Worsted-weight acrylic and sportweight acrylic.
Yarn pictured: Lion Brand® Sayelle (a DuPont certification mark), 3½-oz. skeins, 16 Black #153, 4 Cranberry #180 (color P), 1 each Robin #107 (F), Tile #133 (G), Antique Rose #143 (H), Avocado #173 (J); Lion Brand® Debyshire® Wintuk (a DuPont certification mark), 2-oz. skeins, 1 each Colonial Blue #109 (A), Kelly Green #131 (B), Red #113 (C), White #100 (D), Gold #175 (E).
Other: 16″ pillow form.

Folk flowers made with simple lines and vibrant colors bring this artful afghan to life. For the most dramatic effect, work bright embroideries on a background of black.

TOOLS AND EQUIPMENT

Size G crochet hook, or size to obtain gauge; white tissue paper; tapestry needle.

GAUGE

4 sts = 1″
Square = 15″

DIRECTIONS

Square (make 12): With black, ch 61.

Row 1: Sc in 2nd ch from hook and in each ch across = 60 sc. Ch 1 and turn.

Row 2: Sc in each sc across.

Rep Row 2 until 15″ from beg. Fasten off.

Embroidery: Enlarge embroidery pats and transfer to tissue paper (see placement diagram for number of each motif to make). Center pat on crocheted square. Baste paper pat to square and embroider through paper. Use satin stitch for flowers and leaves and stem stitch for stems. When embroidery is done, tear paper away and tease from under embroidery.

Assembly: Follow diagram for placement of squares. Join cranberry to corner of first square (bottom row, left square) with * sc in corner, ch 7, sl st in same sc (corner lp completed) [ch 7, sk 3 sts (or rows), sc in next st] to next corner, ch 7; rep from * 3 times more, join with sl st to first sc.

Join cranberry to corner of second square (bottom row, center square) with sc in corner, ch 3, sl st in corresponding corner of first square, ch 3, sl st in same sc on second square, [ch 3, sl st in corresponding lp on first square, ch 3, sk 3 sts, sc in next st on second square] to next corner; complete edging in same manner as for first square.

Rep procedure with rem squares.

Edging: Work Rows 1–6 on both ends of afghan.

Row 1: With right side facing and afghan turned to work across a short edge, join cranberry with sc in corner, * ch 7, sc in next lp; rep from * across. Ch 4, turn.

Row 2: * Sc in next lp, ch 7; rep from * across. Ch 4, turn.

Rows 3–6: Rep Row 2. At the end of Row 6, fasten off.

Rep Rows 1–6 on rem end of afghan. Fasten off.

Last rnd: Join cranberry in corner, * 7 sc in corner lp, [5 sc in next lp] to next corner; rep from * 3 times more, join with sl st to first sc. Fasten off.

Pillow: Make 2 squares as for afghan. Embroider 1 square in same manner as for afghan.

Assembly and edging: Rnd 1: With wrong sides facing, work edging through both pieces on 3 sides and through embroidered piece only on rem side. Join cranberry with * sc in corner, ch 7, sl st in same sc (corner lp completed), [ch 7, sk 3 sts, sc in next st] to next corner, ch 7; rep from * 3 times more, join with sl st to first sc.

Rnd 2: Sl st to next lp, * ch 7, sl st in same sc (corner lp completed), [ch 7, sc in next lp] to next corner; rep from * 3 times more, join with sl st to first sc.

Rnd 3: Rep Rnd 2.

Rnd 4: Work * 7 sc in corner lp, [5 sc in next lp] to next corner; rep from * 3 times more. Fasten off.

Insert pillow form and whipstitch opening closed.

1	3	1
REVERSE 3	2	3
REVERSE 3	2	3
1	REVERSE 3	1

Placement Diagram

Each square = 1″.

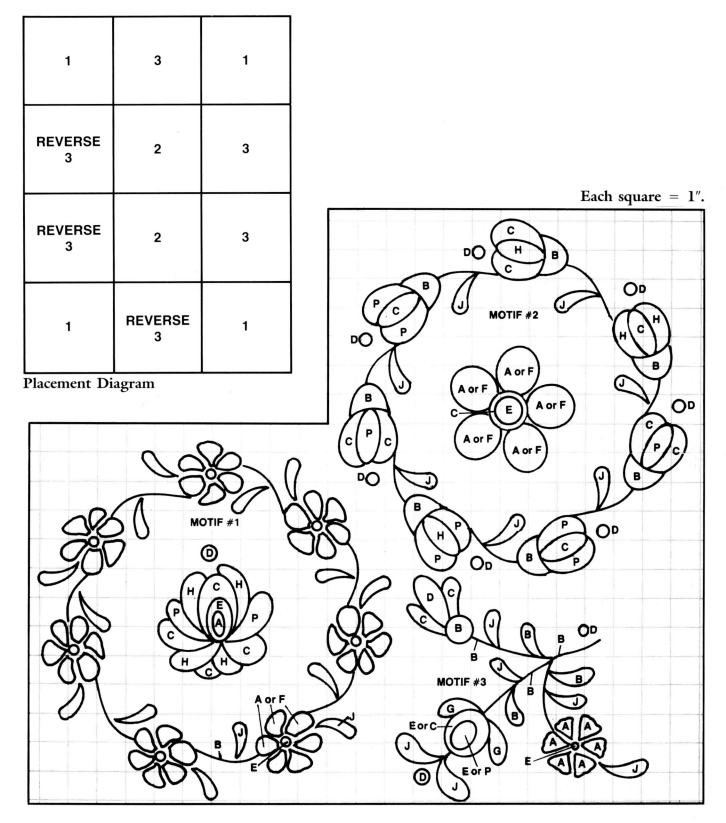

81

Basketweave

FINISHED SIZE
Approximately 46" x 55", not including fringe.

MATERIALS
Yarn description: Worsted-weight acrylic.
Yarn pictured: Bernat® Berella® "4"®, 100-gr. skeins, 7 Pale Sea Green, 4 each Pastel Peach, Medium Brown.

TOOLS AND EQUIPMENT
Size J crochet hook, or size to obtain gauge.

GAUGE
3 dc = 1"

DIRECTIONS
Front post dtr (FPdtr): [Yo hook] 3 times, insert hook from front to back around post of dc 2 rows below, complete st as dtr = 1 FPdtr completed.

Note: Turning ch-3 always counts as 1 dc. There will always be 135 sts (including turning ch) in each row.

Afghan: With green, ch 136.

Row 1: Dc in 3rd ch from hook and in each ch across row = 135 dc counting starting ch. Turn.

Row 2: Ch 3 for first dc, dc in each dc across. Fasten off. Turn.

Row 3: Join peach, ch 3 for first dc, dc in each of next 4 dc, * [FPdtr] 5 times, dc in each of next 15 sts; rep from * to last 10 sts, end with [FPdtr] 5 times, dc in 5 dc. Turn.

Row 4: Ch 3 for first dc, dc in each st across. Fasten off. Turn.

Row 5: Join brown, ch 3 for first dc, dc in each of next 14 sts, * [FPdtr] 5 times, dc in each of next 15 sts; rep from * across row. Turn.

Row 6: Rep row 4.

Rep Rows 3–6 working 2 rows each * green, peach, brown; rep from * until there are 16 brown stripes; end with Rows 5 and 6 green. Fasten off.

Edging: Rnd 1: Right side facing, with afghan turned to work across long edge, join green in corner; ch 3 for first dc, in same corner work dc, ch 2, 2 dc, * working across row edges [ch 1, dc in edge of next row] to next corner, ch 1 *; in corner work 2 dc, ch 2, and 2 dc, ** working across short edge [ch 1, sk 1 st, dc in next st] to next corner, ch 1 **; work corner as before; rep from * to * across next long edge; rep from ** to ** across rem short edge. Join with sl st to top of starting ch-3.

Rnd 2: Ch 4 for first dc and ch 1, * in ch-2 corner work 3 dc, ch 3, 2 dc, sk next dc, [ch 1, dc in next dc] to next corner, ch 1; rep from * around, join with sl st to top of starting ch-4.

Rnd 3: Sc in each dc and ch-1 sp around; work 4 sc in each ch-3 corner. Join with sl st to first sc. Fasten off.

Fringe: Cut 4 (14") strands green for each tassel. Knot one tassel through every other st across ends of afghan. Trim fringe even.

The elongated basketweave stitch gives this afghan its unusual and inviting texture. Mix it with your favorite collectibles for an accent piece at home in many settings.

Log Cabin Afghan

Take a log cabin block along with you to make the most of spare moments in your busy day. With patchwork techniques designed for ease, "build" your own country afghan, a block a day.

FINISHED SIZE
Approximately 48″ x 64″.

MATERIALS
Yarn description: Worsted-weight acrylic blend.
Yarn pictured: (No longer available.) 3-oz. skeins, 4 each Color A, B, C, E; 3 Color D.

TOOLS AND EQUIPMENT
Size I crochet hook, or size to obtain gauge.

GAUGE
10 dc = 3″, 6 rows = 3″

DIRECTIONS
Note: If a color is to be used again on the same rnd, work over it with the next group of sts and pick it up when needed. If a color is not needed again on the same rnd, fasten off and join when needed on a future rnd. To avoid holes when changing colors, bring up new color from under dropped color. Always bring up new color as last yo of old color.

Square 1 (make 24): With color A, ch 6 and join with sl st to form ring.

Rnd 1: Ch 3 for first dc, work 3 dc in ring, yo and draw up a lp in next st, yo and through 2 lps on hook, yo with B and through last 2 lps on hook (color change completed), work 5 dc with B, 5 dc with A, and 5 dc with B, changing colors as before. Join with sl st to top of starting ch-3 = 20 dc (including starting ch).

Rnd 2: With A, ch 3 for first dc, dc in next dc, 5 dc in next dc (corner completed), dc in each of 2 dc; with B, * dc in next 2 dc, 5 dc in next dc for corner, dc in 2 dc *; with A rep from * to *, with B rep from * to *; join with sl st to top of starting ch (4 corners established).

Rnd 3: With A, ch 3 for first dc, dc in 3 dc, 3 dc in next dc for corner, dc in each of next 4 dc, with B * dc in 4 dc, 3 dc in next dc for corner, dc in 4 dc *; with A rep from * to *, with B rep from * to *; join with sl st to top of starting ch.

Rnd 4: With A, ch 3 for first dc, dc in 4 dc, 5 dc in next dc for corner, dc in 5 dc, with B * dc in 5 dc, 5 dc in next st for corner, dc in 5 dc *; with A rep from * to *, with B rep from * to *; join with sl st to top of starting ch.

Rnd 5: With A, ch 3 for first dc, dc in 6 dc, 5 dc in next dc for corner, dc in 7 dc, with B * dc in 7 dc, 5 dc in next st for corner, dc in 7 dc *; with A rep from * to *, with B rep from * to *; join with sl st to top of starting ch.

Rnd 6: With A, ch 3 for first dc, dc in 8 dc, 5 dc in next st for corner, dc in 9 dc, with B * dc in 9 dc, 5 dc in next dc for corner, dc in 9 dc *; with A rep from * to *, with B rep from * to *; join with sl st to top of starting ch. Fasten off.

Square 2 (make 24): *Note:* Square 2 is identical to square 1 except for color arrangement.

With C, ch 6 and join with sl st to form a ring.

Rnd 1: Ch 3 for first dc, work 4 dc in ring, with D work 15 dc in ring, join with sl st to top of starting ch = 20 dc (including starting ch).

Rnds 2 and 3: With C, ch 3 for first dc, following color arrangement as established in previous rnd, work same as square 1, Rnds 2 and 3.

Rnd 4: Work C sts same as square 1, Rnd 4; with D work 6 dc, join E and work to last 6 sts, with D work last 6 sts.

Rnds 5 and 6: Continue in pat with color arrangement as established in previous rnd. At end of last rnd, fasten off.

Assembly: Arrange squares in a 6-square x 8-square checkerboard pat, referring to photograph for position-ing. With right sides up, sc squares tog through back lps only.

Edging: Rnd 1: With right side fac-ing, join C in any corner and ch 3 for first dc, work 4 dc in same corner; * dc evenly to next corner, 5 dc in corner; rep from * twice more; dc evenly across last edge, join with sl st to top of starting ch.

Rnd 2: Ch 3 for first dc, dc in each dc around, work 3 dc in each corner. At end of rnd, join with sl st to top of starting ch.

Rnd 3: Ch 3 for first dc, dc in each dc around, work 5 dc in each corner. At end of rnd, join with sl st to top of starting ch. Fasten off.

Winter

Snowfall

Snowflakes made of lightweight cotton yarn and crochet cotton are appliquéd to a cool blue background. Make extra snowflakes to trim Christmas tree or gifts, or to hang in a winter window.

FINISHED SIZE
Approximately 40″ x 52″.

MATERIALS
Yarn description: Sportweight cotton and mercerized cotton thread.
Yarn pictured: Coats & Clark Red Heart® 100% Cotton Sport Yarn, Art. E.284, 2¼-oz. skeins, 10 Bright Blue #813, 1 White #1; J. & P. Coats "Knit-Cro-Sheen," Art. A.64, 250-yd. ball, 1 White #1.

TOOLS AND EQUIPMENT
Size G crochet hook, or size to obtain gauge; size D crochet hook; size #7 steel crochet hook.

GAUGE
6 sts = 1″

DIRECTIONS
With blue and G hook, ch 168.

Row 1: Sc in 2nd ch from hook, * ch 1, sk 1 ch, sc in next ch; rep from * across, end with sc in last ch = 84 sc with ch-1 between each. Ch 1, turn.

Row 2: Sc in first sc, * sc in next ch-1 sp, ch 1; rep from * across, end with sc in last ch-1 sp, sc in last sc. Ch 1, turn.

Row 3: Sc in first sc, * ch 1, sc in next ch-1 sp; rep from * across, end with ch 1, sc in last sc. Ch 1, turn.

Rep Rows 2 and 3 until 230 rows from beg. Fasten off.

Edging: Rnd 1: With D hook, join blue in any corner, * in corner work sc, ch 2, and sc, sc evenly to next corner; rep from * around as established, join with sl st to first sc.

Rnds 2 and 3: Sl st to ch-2 corner, ch 1, * in ch-2 work sc, ch 2, and sc, sc evenly to next corner; rep from * around as established, join with sl st to first sc.

Rnd 4: Sl st to ch-2 corner, * ch 3 for first dc, in same sp work dc, ch 2, and 2 dc, dc evenly to next corner; rep from * around as established, join with sl st to top of starting ch-3.

Rnds 5–10: Rep Rnds 2–4 twice. At the end of Rnd 10, fasten off.

Rnd 11: Join white in any ch-2 corner, * in ch-2 work sc, ch 2, and sc, sc evenly to next corner; rep from * around as established, join with sl st to first sc.

Rnd 12 (picot edge): Sl st to corner, * in corner work sc, ch 2, and sc, [sc in each of next 4 sc, ch 5, sl st in 5th ch from hook (picot completed)] to next corner; rep from * around as established, join with sl st to first sc. Fasten off.

Snowflakes: Make several of each size snowflake. For large snowflakes, use D hook and Cotton Sport Yarn; for small snowflakes, use #7 steel hook and "Knit-Cro-Sheen."

Rnd 1: Ch 6, in 6th ch from hook, work [dc, ch 2] 5 times, join with sl st to 3rd ch of starting ch-6.

Rnd 2: Ch 10, [tr in next dc, ch 6] 5 times, join with sl st to 4th ch of starting ch-10.

Rnd 3: Sl st in next ch-lp, * ch 7, sk next 4 ch, sl st in next ch, sl st in next tr, [ch 3, sl st in 2nd ch from hook] 3 times, ch 1, sl st in same tr (3-picot group completed), sl st in next ch; rep from * around, end with ch 7, sk next 4 ch, sl st in next ch, sl st in joining of previous rnd, work a 3-picot group, join with sl st in same joining.

Rnd 4: Sl st in 3rd ch of ch-7, * [ch 3, dc in 3rd ch from hook, ch 5, sl st in 5th ch from hook] 3 times, ch 3, dc in 3rd ch from hook, sk next ch, sl st in next ch, [ch 3, sl st in 2nd ch from hook] 5 times, ch 1, sl st in 3rd ch of next ch-7 lp; rep from * around as established, join with sl st. Fasten off.

Rep Rnds 1–4 for each snowflake.

Finishing: Tack snowflakes to afghan as desired (see photograph).

Cat in the Window

Stitch our moonstruck kitten in blue, gray, and black accented with white for a small throw with lots of decorating flair. A matching pillow completes the design.

FINISHED SIZE
Afghan: approximately 45″ square.
Pillow: approximately 14″ square.

MATERIALS
Yarn description: Worsted-weight acrylic.
Yarn pictured: Unger® Utopia®, 100-gr. skeins, 4 Blue #202 (color A), 3 Black #104 (B), 6 Gray #101 (C), 1 White #100 (D).
Other: 14″ pillow form.

TOOLS AND EQUIPMENT
Size G crochet hook, or size to obtain gauge; tapestry needle.

GAUGE
Square = 7″, including border

DIRECTIONS
Note: Working the charts will be easier if yarn is wound on bobbins. If a color is to be used again in 4 sts or less, work over it with the next few sts and pick it up when needed. If a color is not needed for more than 4 sts, drop it to the wrong side of the work and pick up when needed. To avoid holes, bring up new color from under dropped color. Always bring up new color as last yo of old color.

Square 2 (make 4): With C, ch 27.

Row 1: Sc in 2nd ch from hook and each ch across = 26 sc. Ch 1, turn.

Row 2: Sc in each sc across. Ch 1 and turn.

Rows 3–16: Rep Row 2.

Rows 17–30: Follow chart 2. At end of Row 30, fasten off.

Border: Work same as square 1.

Assembly: Beg with square 1 in corner, arrange blocks in a 3-square x 3-square checkerboard pat (see photograph). With right sides up, whipstitch squares tog through front lps only, with black yarn.

Afghan border: Rnd 1: With right side facing, join B in any corner, * work 3 sc in corner sc, sc evenly to next corner; rep from * around, join with sl st to first sc. Fasten off. Turn.

Rnd 2: Join C in any corner, * work 3 sc in corner, sc evenly to next corner; rep from * around, join with sl st to first sc. Ch 1, turn.

Rnd 3: Sc in each sc around, work 3 sc in each corner; join with sl st to first sc. Ch 1, turn.

Rnds 4–9: Rep Rnd 3.

Rnd 10: Sc in each sc around, join with sl st to first sc. Ch 1, turn.

Rnds 11–28: Rep Rnds 2–10.

Rnds 29–33: Rep Rnd 3. At end of Rnd 33, fasten off.

Rnds 34–36: Join A; rep Rnd 3.

Rnd 37: Rep Rnd 10.

Rnds 38–45: Rep Rnd 3.

Rnd 46: Rep Rnd 10.

Rnd 47: Rep Rnd 3. Fasten off.

Rnds 48–49: Join D and rep Rnd 3. Fasten off.

Rnds 50–53: Join B; rep Rnd 3.

Rnd 54: Rep Rnd 10. Fasten off.

Afghan: Square 1 (make 5): With color C, ch 27.

Row 1: Sc in 2nd ch from hook and in each of next 13 ch; with B sc in each of next 7 ch; with C sc in each of next 5 ch (Row 1 of chart 1 completed). Ch 1, turn.

Row 2: Working in sc and following chart 1, work 4 A, 9 B, 4 A, 1 C, 8 A (Row 2 of chart 1 completed). Ch 1 and turn.

Rows 3–30: Continue working chart as established. At end of Row 30, fasten off.

Border: With right side facing, join B in any corner, * work 3 sc in corner, work 24 sc evenly spaced to next corner; rep from * around, join with sl st to first sc. Fasten off.

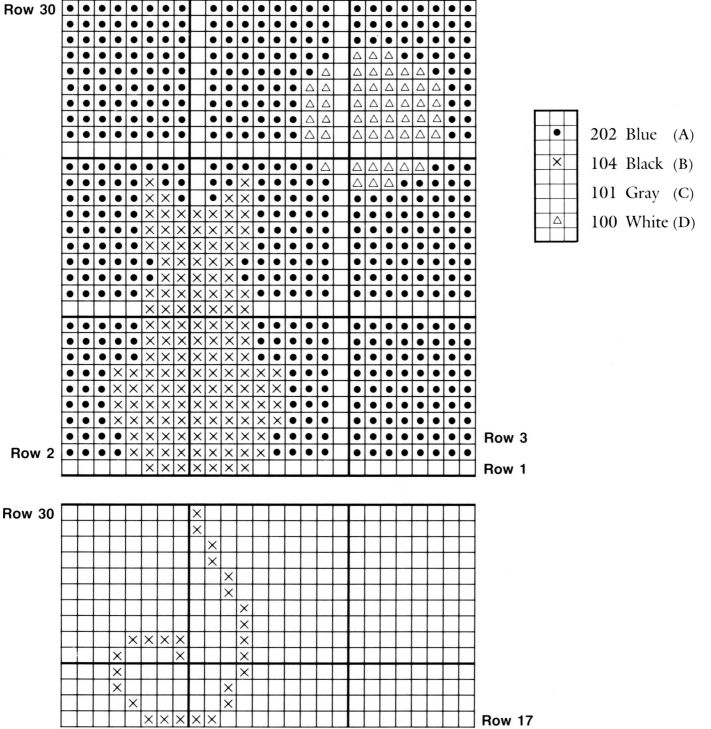

Pillow: Make 4 each of squares 1 and 2. With black yarn, whipstitch tog 2 of each square in same arrangement as for afghan. Rep with rem 4 squares.

With wrong sides facing, sc pillow pieces tog around 3 sides with black yarn. Insert pillow form and sc rem edge tog. Fasten off.

A Cozy Corner

When cold winds blow, you'll love the luxurious warmth of this afghan made with soft brushed yarn. Plush floral centers made of loop stitch are set in squares of a graceful pattern stitch.

FINISHED SIZE
Approximately 50" x 64".

MATERIALS
Yarn description: Worsted-weight brushed acrylic.
Yarn pictured: Unger® Fluffy®, 1¾-oz. balls, 14 Gray (color A), 6 Mauve (B), 3 Peach (C).

TOOLS AND EQUIPMENT
Size H crochet hook, or size to obtain gauge; tapestry needle.

GAUGE
Square = 7"

DIRECTIONS
Square 1 (make 32): With C, ch 6, join with a sl st to form a ring.

Rnd 1: Work 12 sc in ring. Join with sl st to first sc. Ch 1, turn.

Rnd 2 (wrong side): Lp yarn over index finger of left hand from front to back, insert hook in sc, pick up lp under finger, draw through, complete as a sc (lp st completed), work another lp st in same st, work 2 lp sts in each st around, join with sl st to first sc = 24 lp sts. Ch 1, turn.

Rnd 3 (right side): (Keep all lps on right side of work and be careful not to catch lps in sts.) * Sc in next st, 2 sc in next st; rep from * around, join with sl st to first sc = 36 sc. Ch 1 and turn.

Rnd 4: Work 1 lp st in each st around, join with sl st to first sc. Fasten off. Turn.

Rnd 5: Join A, ch 3 for first dc, in same st work 2 dc, * [ch 1, sk 2 sts, 3 dc in next st] twice, ch 1, sk 2 sts, 3 dc in next st, ch 1, and 3 dc (corner completed); rep from * twice more, end with [ch 1, sk 2 sts, 3 dc in next st] twice, ch 1, 3 dc in same st as starting ch, ch 2, join with sl st to 3rd ch of starting ch-3 (4 corners completed).

Rnd 6: Ch 3 for first dc, 2 dc in same sp as starting ch, * [ch 1, 3 dc in next ch-1 sp] 3 times, ch 1, 3 dc in next ch-1 corner, ch 1, and 3 dc; rep from * twice more, end with [ch 1, 3 dc in next ch-1 sp] 3 times, ch 1, 3 dc in same sp as starting ch, ch 1, join with sl st to top of starting ch-3.

Rnd 7: Ch 3 for first dc, 2 dc in same sp as starting ch, * [ch 1, 3 dc in next ch-1 sp] 4 times, ch 1, 3 dc in next ch-1 corner, ch 1, and 3 dc; rep from * twice more, end with [ch 1, 3 dc in next ch-1 sp] 4 times, ch 1, 3 dc in same sp as starting ch, ch 1, join with sl st to top of starting ch-3.

Rnd 8: Ch 3 for first dc, 2 dc in same sp as starting ch, * [ch 1, 3 dc in next ch-1 sp] 5 times, ch 1, 3 dc in next ch-1 corner, ch 1, and 3 dc; rep from * twice more, end with [ch 1, 3 dc in next ch-1 sp] 5 times, ch 1, 3 dc in same sp as starting ch, ch 1, join with sl st to top of starting ch-3. Fasten off.

Rnd 9: Join B in any ch-1 corner, * 3 sc in corner, [sc in each dc] to corner; rep from * 3 times more, join with sl st to first sc. Fasten off.

Square 2 (make 31): Work the same as square 1, substituting B for C at center.

Assembly: Beg with square 1 in corner, arrange squares in a 7-square x 9-square checkerboard pat. With right sides up, whipstitch squares tog through back lps only. Leave a sc unworked before and after each corner for a small opening at intersections.

Edging: Rnd 1: With right side facing, join B in corner, * work 3 sc in corner, sc in each st to next corner; rep from * 3 times more, join with sl st to first sc.

Rnd 2: Sc in each sc around, work 3 sc in each corner. Join with sl st.

Rnd 3: Working from left to right, ch 3 for first hdc and ch 1, sk 1 st, * hdc in next st, ch 1, sk 1 st; rep from * around. Join with sl st to 2nd ch of starting ch. Fasten off.

Toss a Throw

Looking for a gift idea that's pretty and practical? Toss off one—or more—of these lovely throws. These simple designs can be made quickly and will bring great pleasure to your friends!

Faded-Rose Throw

FINISHED SIZE
30″ x 50″, not including fringe.

MATERIALS
Yarn description: Worsted-weight brushed acrylic.
Yarn pictured: Brunswick® Windmist Orlon®, 50-gr. skeins, 9 Faded Rose #2824.

TOOLS AND EQUIPMENT
Size K crochet hook, or size to obtain gauge.

GAUGE
2 sts = 1″

DIRECTIONS
Ch 102 to measure 50″.

    Row 1: Hdc in 3rd ch from hook and in each ch across = 101 sts including starting ch. Ch 1, turn.

    Row 2: Sc in each hdc across. Ch 2, turn.

    Row 3: Hdc in each sc across. Ch 1, turn.

    Rep Rows 2 and 3 until 30″ from beg. Fasten off.

Fringe: Cut 2 (12″) strands for each tassel. Knot a tassel through every other st on each end of the throw.

White Throw

FINISHED SIZE
30″ x 50″.

MATERIALS
Yarn description: Worsted-weight brushed mohair blend.
Yarn pictured: Classic Elite LaGran Mohair, 1½-oz. skeins, 9 White.

TOOLS AND EQUIPMENT
Size K crochet hook, or size to obtain gauge.

GAUGE
5 sts = 2″

DIRECTIONS
Ch 126 sts to measure 50″.

    Row 1: Sc in 2nd ch from hook and each ch across = 125 sc. Ch 1 and turn.

    Row 2: Sc in each sc across. Ch 1 and turn.

    Rep Row 2 until 30″ from beg. Fasten off.

Stripe It Rich

FINISHED SIZE
Approximately 40″ x 76″.

MATERIALS
Yarn description: Worsted-weight machine-washable wool.

Yarn pictured: Scheepjeswol® Superwash Plus, 50-gr. balls, 30 each Camel #4825, Teal Blue #4838, Rose #4849, Khaki Green #4848, Wine #4824, Forest Green #4816.

TOOLS AND EQUIPMENT
Size G crochet hook; tapestry needle.

DIRECTIONS
Note: Square is worked on the diagonal. Work the first half of each square in one color and the remaining half in five rows each of the other colors in random order. Be sure to use all the colors in equal amounts on a rotating basis so that you will not use up one color faster than another.

Square: Ch 3.

Row 1: Sc in 2nd ch from hook and in next ch = 2 sc. Ch 1, turn.

Row 2: Work 2 sc in each sc across = 4 sc. Ch 1, turn.

Row 3: Work 2 sc in first sc, sc in 2 sc, 2 sc in last sc = 6 sc. Ch 1, turn.

Row 4: Work 2 sc in first sc, sc to last sc, 2 sc in last sc. Ch 1, turn.

Rep Row 4 until there are 50 sts. Work 1 row even in sc.

Next row: Join new color and draw up a lp in each of first 2 sc, yo and through 3 lps on hook (1 sc dec at beg of row completed), sc to last 2 sc, draw up a lp in each of last 2 sc, yo and through 3 lps on hook (1 sc dec at end of row completed).

Dec 1 st each edge until all sts are worked off. Remember to change colors every five rows when working the second half of each square.

Continue making squares until all yarn is used.

Assembly: With wrong sides facing and working through inner lps only, use matching yarn to join all the squares tog in random order. Or use the photograph as a guide to create our diamond pattern.

Here's the perfect take-along project. Pack your yarn tote with jewel colors and, as you have time, crochet squares of bold diagonal stripes. Join them for a throw that's diamond-bright.

Fisherman's Afghan

FINISHED SIZE
Approximately 45″ x 60″, not including fringe.

MATERIALS
Yarn description: Worsted-weight acrylic.
Yarn pictured: (No longer available; see suggested substitute below.) Talon American Dawn Sayelle (a DuPont certification mark), 3-oz. skeins, 13 Fisherman.
Substitute: Caron® Dawn Sayelle (a DuPont certification mark), in color of choice.

TOOLS AND EQUIPMENT
Size K crochet hook, or size to obtain gauge.

GAUGE
3 sts = 1″

DIRECTIONS
Ch 154.

Row 1: Dc in 3rd ch from hook and in each ch across = 152 dc including starting ch. Turn.

Row 2 (wrong side): Ch 3 for first dc, * yo and insert hook around the post of dc directly below, yo and complete as dc (front post dc completed); rep from * across to last st, dc in turning ch. Turn.

Row 3: Ch 3 for first dc, dc in each of next 3 dc, count back 3 dc on previous row, yo, and drawing up long lp, complete as a dc (long diagonal dc completed), * dc in each of next 3 dc, count back 3 dc, work a long diagonal dc; rep from * across, end with dc in last st. Turn.

Row 4: Ch 3 for first dc, * sk long diagonal dc, dc in each of next 3 dc, turn, count back 3 sts, work long diagonal dc at base of long diagonal dc of previous row, turn; rep from * across, end with dc in last dc. (*Note:* Each set of long diagonal dc of Rows 2 and 3 forms a sideways V.) Turn.

Row 5: Ch 3 for first dc, dc in each dc across, sk all long diagonal dc. Turn.

Rep Rows 2–5 a total of 15 times. Fasten off.

Fringe: Cut 5 (16″) strands of yarn for each tassel. Knot tassels about 1″ apart across both ends of afghan. Make a 2nd row of knots in fringe by knotting tog 5 strands from one tassel and 5 from the next tassel about ½″ below the first knot.

In this V-stitch afghan, you can use simple techniques to achieve impressive results. Double crochet worked in lengthwise panels with a large hook gives the raised look of Aran knitting.

Lace & Linens

Take a color cue for this luxurious angora afghan from your favorite linens. Match an embroidered accent or a lovely printed pattern with a lacy afghan in the same rich hue.

FINISHED SIZE
Approximately 42" x 50".

MATERIALS
Yarn description: Sportweight, 70% angora, 30% wool.
Yarn pictured: Laines Anny Blatt Angor' Anny, 20-gr. balls, 20 Prune #1501.
Alternate: Laines Anny Blatt Angora Super, Art. 21209, Bourgogne #2814.

TOOLS AND EQUIPMENT
Sizes G and H crochet hooks.

DIRECTIONS
Note: Pat st is a multiple of 10, plus 9.

V st: Work 2 dc, ch 2, and 2 dc all in same st.

Afghan: With H hook, ch 150 loosely.
  Row 1: Hdc in 3rd ch from hook, hdc in each ch across; 149 hdc. Turn.
  Row 2: Ch 3 for first dc, dc in next st, sk 2 sts, * V st, ch 5, sk 4 sts, sc in next st, turn, ch 3, 5 dc under last ch-5, turn, ch 3 (counts as first dc), 1 dc in next 5 dc (6 dc with ch 3), sk 4 sts; rep from * across, end with V st in next st, sk 2 sts, 1 dc in each of 2 sts = 14 large motifs. Turn.
  Rows 3–5: Ch 3 for first dc, dc in next dc, * V st under ch-2 of next V st, ch 9; rep from * across, end with V st under ch-2 of V st, 1 dc in each of 2 sts. Turn.
  Row 6: Ch 3 for first dc, dc in next st, * V st under ch-2 of V st, ch 5, go down to first dc of large motif and work a sc going over and catching the 3 loose ch-9, turn, ch 3, 5 dc under

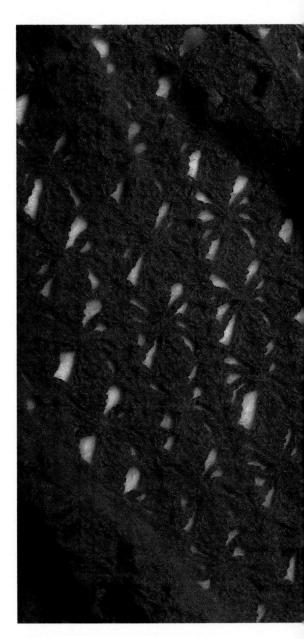

ch-5 (start of a new large motif), turn, ch 3 for first dc, dc in next 5 dc = 6 dc total; rep from * across, end with V st under ch-2 of V st, 1 dc in each of 2 dc. Turn.
  Rep Rows 3–6 for pat. Work even until 50" from beg or desired length. End with Row 6. Ch 3, turn.
  Next row: Dc in next st, * V st

102

under ch-2 of V st, ch 4, sc in 6th st of large motif, ch 4; rep from * across, end with V st under ch-2 of V st, 1 dc in each of last 2 sts. Turn.

Last row: Ch 2 for first hdc, hdc in next dc, * 1 hdc in next 2 dc of V st, hdc in each of 4 ch, hdc in sc, 1 hdc in each of 4 ch; rep from * across, end with 1 hdc in last 2 dc. Fasten off.

Edging: With G hook, join yarn to starting ch corner.

Rnd 1: With right side facing and, working backwards along starting ch from left to right, * ch 1, hdc in first st, [ch 1, sk 1, hdc in next st] to corner, ch 3 at corner; rep from * around. Join with a sl st. Fasten off.

Poinsettias Bloom

This showpiece afghan will highlight your holidays for years to come. Arrange bright cross-stitch poinsettias on a background of snowy white and border them with panels of textured evergreen.

FINISHED SIZE
Approximately 58" x 67".

MATERIALS
Yarn description: Worsted-weight acrylic.
Yarn pictured: (No longer available; see suggested substitute below.) Coats & Clark Red Heart® "Preference," Art. E.270, 3½-oz. skeins, 11 White #1, 5 Emerald #673, 3 Jockey Red #904, 1 each Green Apple #667, Dark Gold #606, Yellow #231.
Substitute: Coats & Clark Red Heart® 4-Ply Handknitting Yarn, Art. E.267, White #1, Emerald #676, Jockey Red #902, Mint Julep #669, Dark Gold #602, Yellow #230.

TOOLS AND EQUIPMENT
Size H afghan hook, or size to obtain gauge; size H crochet hook; tapestry needle.

GAUGE
7 sts = 2", 3 rows = 1" (afghan st)

DIRECTIONS
Afghan st: Row 1: *Step 1:* Keeping all lps on hook, draw up a lp through top lp only, in 2nd ch from hook and each ch across = same number of lps as chs. Do not turn.

Step 2: Yo and draw through first lp on hook, * yo and through 2 lps on hook; rep from * across (1 lp rem on hook for the first lp of next row). Do not turn.

Row 2: *Step 1:* Keeping all lps on hook, draw up a lp from under 2nd vertical bar, * draw up a lp from under next vertical bar; rep from * across. Do not turn.

Step 2: Rep Step 2 of Row 1.
Rep both steps of Row 2 for number of afghan st rows specified.

Cable panels (make 4): With afghan hook and emerald, ch 9.
Rows 1–3: Work in afghan st.
Row 4 (cable row): Draw up a lp from under each of next 3 bars of previous row for 4 lps on hook; [yo hook] 3 times, draw up a lp from under 2nd bar of row 2 rows below, [yo and through 2 lps on hook] 3 times for 5 lps on hook, [yo hook] 3 times, draw up a lp from under next to last bar of row 2 rows below, [yo and through 2 lps on hook] 4 times for 5 lps on hook (cable completed); holding cable to front of work, draw up a lp from under each of last 4 bars of previous row for 9 lps on hook. End by rep Row 2, Step 2 of afghan st.
Row 5: Work even in afghan st.
Rep Rows 4 and 5 until 183 rows from beg.
Row 184: Sl st in each vertical bar across. Fasten off.

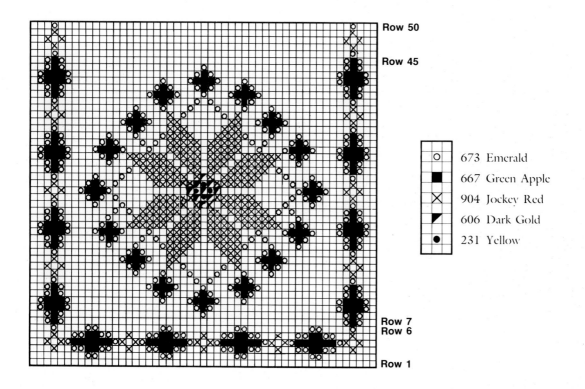

Row 50
Row 45

Row 7
Row 6

Row 1

O	673 Emerald
■	667 Green Apple
X	904 Jockey Red
◤	606 Dark Gold
●	231 Yellow

Cross-stitch panels (make 3): With afghan hook and white, ch 52. Work in afghan st until 183 rows from beg.

Row 184: Sl st in each vertical bar across. Fasten off.

Work the cross-stitch design on each of the 3 panels according to the chart. Work Rows 1–6 of the chart, beg at the bottom of each panel, then rep Rows 7–50 three times, work Rows 7–45 once; end by working from Row 6 to Row 1.

Assembly: With wrong sides facing, join red with crochet hook and sc panels tog, alternating cable panels and cross-stitch panels.

Edging: Rnd 1: Right side facing, with crochet hook, join red with sc in any corner, in same corner work ch 1, and sc, * sc evenly to next corner, in corner work sc, ch 1, and sc; rep from * twice more, sc evenly across to last corner, join with sl st to first sc.

Rnd 2: Sl st to ch-1 corner, * in corner work sc, ch 2, and sc, [ch 1, sk 1 sc, sc in next sc] to next corner, ch 1; rep from * twice more, [ch 1, sk 1 sc, sc in next sc] to last corner, ch 1, join with sl st to first sc. Fasten off.

Rnd 3: Join emerald with sc to ch-2 sp in corner; in same corner work ch 2 and sc, * [sc in next ch-1 sp, ch 1] to next corner, sc in ch-1 sp before corner, in corner work sc, ch 2, and sc; rep from * twice more, [sc in next ch-1 sp, ch 1] across to last corner, sc in ch-1 sp before last corner, join with sl st to first sc.

Rnd 4: Sl st to ch-2 corner, in corner work sc, ch 2, and sc, * [ch 1, sc in next ch-1 sp] to next corner, ch 1, in corner work sc, ch 2, and sc; rep from * around as established, join with sl st to first sc.

Rnd 5: Rep Rnd 3. Fasten off.
Rnd 6: Join red and rep Rnd 4.
Rnd 7: Rep Rnd 3. Fasten off.

Christmas Ribbons

FINISHED SIZE

Approximately 40"x 50".

MATERIALS

Yarn description: Bulky-weight wool blend.

Yarn pictured: (No longer available; see suggested substitute below.) Phildar #130 Kadische, 50-gr. skeins, 20 Blanc #10.

Substitute: Phildar #150 Boeing, Blanc #10.

Other: Christmas-stripe ribbon (1¼" wide), 3 yd.; red grosgrain ribbon (1" wide), 3 yd.; green grosgrain ribbon (1" wide), 3 yd.

TOOLS AND EQUIPMENT

Size K crochet hook.

DIRECTIONS

Ch 106 loosely.

Row 1: Tr in 5th ch from hook and in each ch across = 103 sts including starting ch. Turn.

Row 2: Ch 5 for first tr, * ch 1, sk 1 tr, tr in next tr; rep from * across. Turn.

Row 3: Ch 4 for first tr, tr in each ch-1 and tr across. Turn.

Row 4: Ch 4 for first tr, tr in each tr across. Turn.

Rows 5–7: Rep Rows 2–4.

Row 8: Rep Row 2.

Rows 9–35: Rep Row 4.

Rows 36–41: Rep Rows 2–4 twice.

Row 42: Rep Row 2.

Row 43: Rep Row 3. Fasten off.

Edging: Join yarn in any corner and work around afghan in reverse sc. At end of rnd, join with sl st to first sc. Fasten off.

Finishing: Working colors as desired, weave ribbons through filet rows (Row 2). Tack ends of ribbons to afghan to secure.

Trim with ribbons to suit the season: rosy red for Valentine's; green for St. Patrick's Day; and, in July, red, white, and blue.

Crochet Craft

In crochet, just a little craft (or know-how) will reward you with hours of pleasant stitchery and lovely handcrafted pieces you'll be proud to share. Join in the fun with this quick review of basic techniques.

CHOOSING MATERIALS AND TOOLS

One of the great appeals of crochet is the simplicity of the required supplies. All you really need is a hook and yarn to take part in this enjoyable craft.

A Choice of Yarn

Crochet can be done with anything from the finest cotton thread—used to make delicate edgings for linens—to strips of fabric worked into rugs or baskets. Afghans generally are made from natural or synthetic yarns, categorized by weight as follows:

fingering yarn: lightweight yarn used for baby things or other very delicate pieces.

sportweight yarn: a medium-weight yarn used for light garments and afghans.

worsted-weight yarn: heaviest of the standard weights. Worsted-weight yarns are used for many of the afghans in this book.

bulky yarn: very heavyweight yarn, about twice as thick as worsted-weight yarn.

Substituting Yarns

Instructions for the afghans in this book in most cases specify the particular yarn used to make each piece. When the original yarn is no longer available, we've suggested a substitute that should work well. We've also given a generic description of the original yarn to guide you in making the substitute of your choice. To obtain the same effects as in the pictured afghan, use the same yarn, or pick a substitute that is in the same weight category and is made of the same fiber.

If you substitute another yarn for the original, be aware that you may need a somewhat different amount. Yarn is sold by weight (by the 2-ounce skein or 50-gram ball, for example), but is worked by the yard. Two ounces of one worsted-weight yarn may yield a different yardage from two ounces of another worsted-weight. A knowledgeable yarn shop staff can be of great help in finding a successful substitute and in advising you of the proper amount to buy. Another helpful source of information is Maggie Righetti's *Universal Yarn Finder* (New York: Prentice Hall Press, 1987), which contains conversion charts for many popular yarns. If, after consulting these sources, you still have questions about the amount of substitute yarn to purchase, measure off 20 yards of the yarn you plan to use, work a pattern swatch (making sure to use the correct gauge—more about that later), and use the size of the finished swatch and the finished size of the piece as given in the instructions to help you estimate the yardage you will need.

In any case, you should always plan to buy a bit more yarn than you think will be required to finish any project, since yarn color is dependent on dye lot, and a later purchase of the same yarn may vary slightly in color. Your yarn shop may allow you to exchange unopened skeins for credit; check when you buy.

Crochet Hooks

The smallest crochet hooks are made of steel and are used to work very fine threads into lacy edgings, doilies, and other delicate pieces. Afghans are worked with larger aluminum or plastic hooks, sized B (the smallest) through K (the largest). Oversized wooden or plastic hooks are available for use with heavy yarns or to obtain special effects.

In the instructions for each project you'll find a recommended-size hook; however, you may need a size larger or smaller than specified, depending upon the tension with which you crochet, so plan to have a range of sizes on hand.

Afghan hooks are made especially for working the afghan stitch. They have shafts long enough to hold all the stitches in an individual row and a metal cap at the end to prevent the stitches from slipping off.

Other Supplies

You'll need a small pair of scissors and some tapestry needles. A ruler or knitters' gauge measure is handy for checking gauge. And you may want to include tiny safety pins or other stitch markers among your equipment.

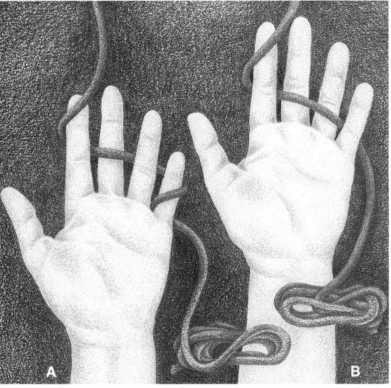

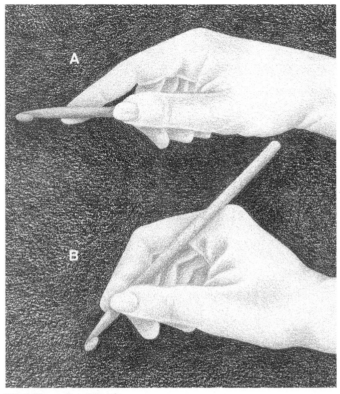

Holding the Yarn
The left hand controls the yarn. Weave the yarn through the fingers of the left hand in the way that is more comfortable to you. Some people like to wrap the little finger for extra control of the yarn (A); some do not (B). In either case, the forefinger plays the most important role in regulating tension, as yarn is fed to the work.

Holding the Hook
The right hand makes the stitches. Hold the hook as you would a piece of chalk (A) or a pencil (B). If your hook has a finger rest, position your thumb and opposing finger there for extra control.

LEARNING THE BASIC TECHNIQUES
Like the basic materials of crochet, the basic techniques are very simple. All you'll need to begin are a few easy lessons and a few hours of practice.

How to Hold the Hook
The best hand position for making crochet is a very individual choice. In time, your hands will "tell" you where they need to be in order to achieve the effects you want. But in the beginning, try to learn the most commonly recommended hand positions.

   Note to left-handed crocheters: Since instructions for crocheted projects most often appear with right-handed instructions only, it may be worth your while to try to learn right-handed techniques for crochet. Actually, since the work is shared between the hands even in "right-handed" crochet, it may be surprisingly easy for you to make use of the accompanying diagrams. If working in this way is not comfortable, use a mirror to reverse these diagrams and the stitch diagrams that appear on the following pages.

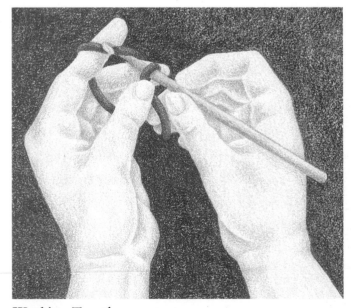

Working Together
Once work has begun, the thumb and middle finger of the left hand come into play, pressing together to hold the stitches just made.

110

Slip Knot Diagram

Loop the yarn around and let the loose end of the yarn fall behind the loop to form a pretzel shape as shown. Insert the hook (A) and pull both ends to close the knot (B). Careful—not too tight!

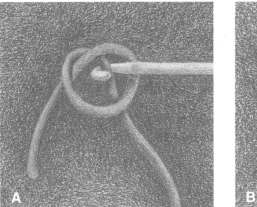

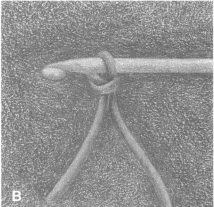

Making a Slip Knot

The slip knot is the first movement of every crochet project; its purpose is to attach the yarn to the hook. With a little practice, it will become second nature.

Making a Chain

The chain stitch is used to establish a foundation for a crocheted piece. Make the individual chain stitch as shown below. Then try making a long chain. With practice, you will achieve a flowing, even movement and produce chains that are the same size and evenly spaced. Try to work with moderate tension, making stitches that are neither very loose nor very tight.

Crochet patterns usually begin with the instruction to make a foundation chain with a certain number of chain stitches. (*Note:* Never count the loop remaining on the hook as a chain.) When you are counting a long chain, it's easy to lose your place. Try marking every twentieth chain with a small safety pin or a snippet of contrasting yarn; if you lose count, you won't have to start again at the beginning.

Once you can make an even chain, you are ready to learn the basic stitches. (Don't worry if the chain twists and curls a bit; it should straighten out as you work rows of stitches into it.)

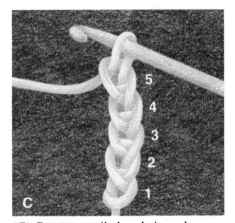

Chain Stitch Diagram

(A) Place a slip knot on your hook. With hands in the position shown at left, and with the thumb and middle finger of the left hand holding the yarn end, wrap the yarn up and over the hook. This movement is called "yarn over (yo)" and is basic to every crochet stitch.

(B) Use the hook to pull the yarn through the loop (lp) already on the hook. The combination of yo and pulling the yarn through the lp makes one chain stitch (ch).

(C) Repeat until the ch is as long as you wish, trying to keep the movement even and relaxed, and all the ch stitches (sts) the same size. As you work, move your left thumb and middle finger up the ch, holding it near the working area. Otherwise it will twist and you will lose control of the work. Count sts as shown in diagram.

LEARNING THE BASIC STITCHES

Single Crochet

Single crochet (sc) is the shortest basic crochet stitch. Used alone, it produces a dense, firm fabric.

Double Crochet

Double crochet (dc) is a longer stitch (twice as long as single crochet) and produces a softer, more drapable fabric.

Half Double Crochet

Half double crochet (hdc) is between single crochet and double crochet in size.

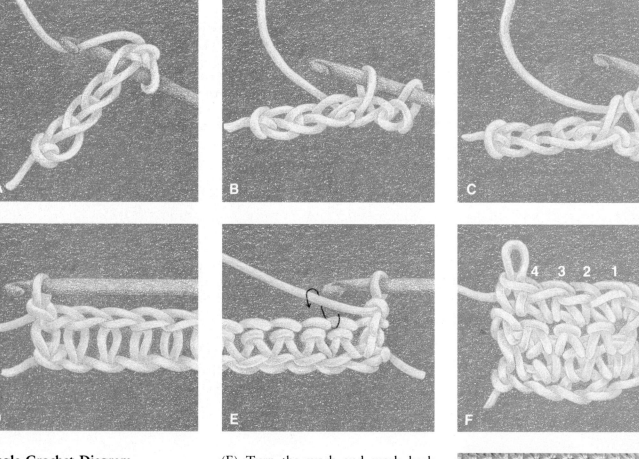

Single Crochet Diagram

(A) Insert hook under top 2 lps of 2nd ch from hook. (Always work sts through 2 lps unless instructions specify otherwise.)

(B) Yo and pull yarn through ch (2 lps on hook).

(C) Yo and pull yarn through 2 lps on hook (1 sc completed).

(D) Continue across row, working 1 sc into each ch of the foundation ch. When you have completed the row (Row 1), make a turning ch.

(E) Turn the work and work back across the row, working a sc into each sc to complete Row 2.

(F) Counting sc sts is a bit more difficult than counting ch sts. Study this diagram until you can see the individual sts.

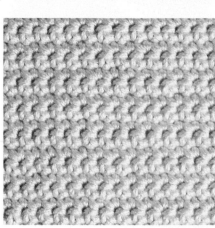

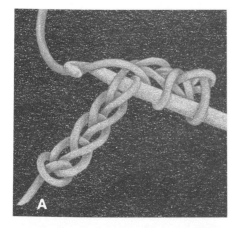

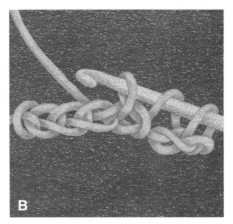

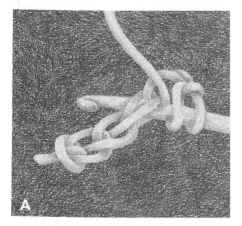

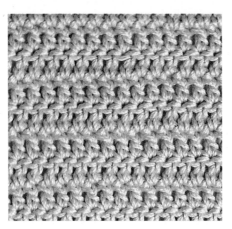

Double Crochet Diagram

(A) Yo, insert hook into 4th ch from hook and yo.

(B) Pull yarn through ch (3 lps on hook).

(C) Yo and pull yarn through 2 lps on hook (2 lps remaining).

(D) Yo and pull yarn through 2 remaining (rem) lps (1 dc completed).

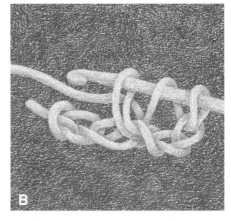

Half Double Crochet Diagram

(A) Yo, insert hook into 3rd ch from hook.

(B) Yo and pull yarn through ch (3 lps on hook).

(C) Yo and pull yarn through 3 lps on hook (1 hdc completed).

Triple (or Treble) Crochet

Triple crochet (tr) is longer than double crochet and makes a flexible, open fabric.

Double Triple (or Double Treble) Crochet

Double triple crochet (dtr) is even longer than triple crochet.

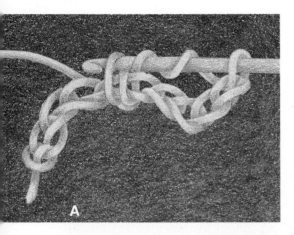

Triple Crochet Diagram

(A) Yo twice, insert hook into 5th ch from hook. Yo and pull yarn through ch (4 lps on hook).

(B) Yo, pull yarn through 2 lps on hook (3 lps rem). Yo, pull yarn through 2 lps on hook (2 lps rem). Yo, pull yarn through 2 lps on hook (1 tr completed).

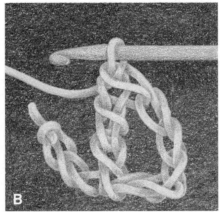

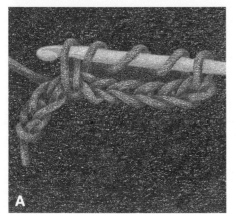

Double Triple Crochet Diagram

(A) Yo 3 times, insert hook into 6th ch from hook. Yo, pull yarn through ch (5 lps on hook).

(B) Yo, pull yarn through 2 lps at a time. Repeat (rep) this motion a total of 4 times (1 dtr completed).

Stitch	Working into foundation ch, turn and begin in	At end of each row	Start next row by inserting hook in
Single Crochet (sc)	2nd ch from hook	ch 1, turn	1st st
Half Double Crochet (hdc)	3rd ch from hook	ch 2, turn	1st st
Double Crochet (dc)	4th ch from hook	ch 3, turn	2nd st
Triple Crochet (tr)	5th ch from hook	ch 4, turn	2nd st
Double Triple Crochet (dtr)	6th ch from hook	ch 5, turn	2nd st

When you can work all these stitches comfortably and consistently, you have mastered the basic "vocabulary" of crochet. It is the combination and placement of these elementary stitches that give each crocheted design its individual character. The key to that character is found in each design's set of instructions; but before we can talk about reading instructions, there are just a few more basic techniques—or ways of working—to review.

Working in Rows

Many crocheted pieces are worked back and forth in rows. Row 1 is worked right to left into the foundation row of chain stitches; then the work is turned and continued with Row 2 worked back across the row of preceding stitches. Whenever the work is turned, a "turning chain" of a given number of chain stitches must be made in order to raise the new row to the proper height.

To compensate for the space taken up by a turning chain, the first stitch of a new row is sometimes worked not into the first stitch of the row below, as you might expect, but into the second stitch, depending on the size of the stitch being worked.

At the end of the row, the final stitch is usually worked into the top of the previous turning chain. Insert your hook so that two loops of the turning chain are above the hook, yarn over, and proceed with the stitch as usual.

If the turning chain is not used correctly, you will not be able to maintain the correct number of stitches in the row, and the edges of the piece will become uneven. The chart at the top of this page gives *general* guidelines for the correct number of chains for each turning chain and the proper placement for the initial stitch in each row.

(*Note:* Be sure to check individual instructions for each afghan; these general rules are sometimes altered for special stitches or to create special effects.)

Working in Rounds

Some crochet designs (granny squares and other medallion-style designs, for example) are worked in the round. One way to begin work in the round is to make a foundation chain and join the last and first chains into a ring with a slip stitch. *Note:* Don't confuse this with the slip knot used to attach the yarn to the hook.

Slip Stitch Diagram
Here a slip stitch (sl st) is used to join a ring. Taking care not to twist ch, insert hook into first ch, yo, and pull yarn through ch and lp on hook (sl st completed).

Adding Yarn

When your ball of yarn runs out and you must add more, or if you encounter a break in the yarn (or a yarn imperfection that must be cut out), you will need to know how to join in new yarn. In general, it is preferable to join new yarn at the end of a row, but with the right techniques it's possible to join new yarn neatly in the middle of the row, too. See explanations for both techniques under "Exploring Color" below. Techniques for changing yarn at the row's end or along the row are the same, whether you are joining a new color of yarn or simply a new ball of the same color yarn (although special care must be taken to preserve the pattern when you are making a color change as well as masking a break in the yarn).

Removing Mistakes

In general, smooth yarns can be easily and quickly unraveled back to the point of error if you notice a mistake and decide to "erase" and try again. Mohair, which tangles easily, may be more difficult to unravel.

Fastening Off

To end a piece or section, cut the yarn, leaving a six-inch "tail." Yarn over and pull the loose end through the last loop on the hook. Thread the loose end into a tapestry needle and weave it carefully into the back of the work.

WORKING FROM INSTRUCTIONS

Once you've mastered the basic techniques of crochet, you're ready to make all sorts of wonderful projects by following the pattern instructions. Don't be afraid of the instructions; they're really much less mysterious than they appear.

Reading and Understanding Instructions

Each set of crochet instructions is like a "recipe" for the illustrated piece. And like recipes, crochet instructions are usually printed in abbreviated form, to save space. The special "code" that results can appear more difficult than it really is: while most of us, in trying out a new dish, can face a *tsp* or a *Tbl* without so much as a blink, the sight of *ch 1, * sk 1 sc, dc in next sc, ch 3,*

sl st in top of dc (picot), rep from * across can strike terror in the heart of the new crocheter!

Familiarity is the key to working crochet instructions with ease. Take some time to familiarize yourself with the common abbreviations listed below, and with the punctuation marks—asterisks and brackets—used to group instructions into working units.

Take instructions one row at a time—you can even copy instructions for each row onto a separate index card, if that will help organize your approach. Remember that with each set of instructions you work through, your confidence in reading printed instructions will increase.

beg	begin(ning)
ch	chain
ch-	refers to chain previously made
dc	double crochet
dec	decrease(s) (d) (ing)
dtr	double triple crochet
hdc	half double crochet
inc	increase(s) (d) (ing)
lp(s)	loop(s)
pat(s)	pattern(s)
rem	remain(s) (ing)
rep	repeat
rnd(s)	round(s)
sc	single crochet
sk	skip
sl st	slip stitch
sp(s)	space(s)
st(s)	stitch(es)
tog	together
tr	triple crochet
yo	yarn over

Repeat whatever follows * as indicated. Work directions given in brackets the number of times specified.

"Work even" means to work in stitch or pattern with no increases or decreases.

Instructional Charts

Sometimes instructions are supplemented by charts or diagrams. Diagrams may show how to accomplish an unusual stitch or other maneuver, or may show how pieces of a project are to be assembled. Charts are usually a stitch-by-stitch, row-by-row representation of a design section of the piece, showing different stitches to be used, color patterning, or both.

Charts show the right side of the piece. Since you must work back and forth across the rows of the piece, you must learn to "read" back and forth across the chart as well. Read Row 1 right to left, just as it is worked. Read Row 2 left to right, Row 3 right to left, and so on. (*Note:* Charts worked in afghan stitch are a bit different; each row of the chart must be read from right to left and then left to right to properly complete the stitch.)

One special technique always represented by a chart is that of filet crochet. Filet crochet is essentially a crocheted mesh, made of chain stitches and double crochet, with design areas filled by double crochet. (On our charts, these filled design areas are represented by shaded squares.) The number of chains and double crochet stitches used to construct each square of the mesh varies from design to design; exact numbers to use are given in each set of instructions.

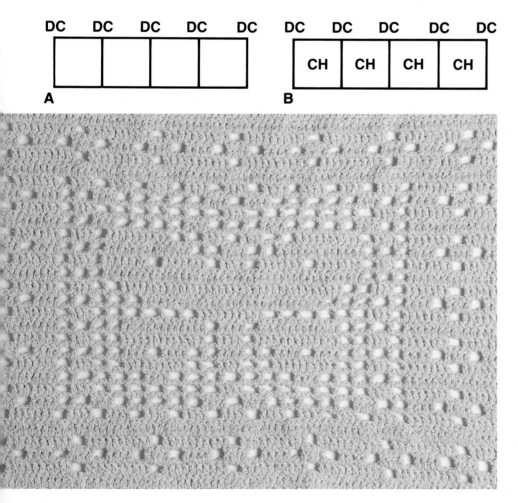

A — DC DC DC DC DC

B — DC DC DC DC DC / CH CH CH CH

C — DC DC DC DC DC / DC DC DC DC

Filet Crochet Diagram

(A) Each vertical line represents a dc (although the first dc in the row is replaced by a turning ch).

(B) The horizontal line of each open square is made by 1 or more ch.

(C) Each filled space (sp) (shaded square on chart) is accomplished by working 1 or more additional dc between the 2 dc that form the vertical edges of the square. Work the extra dc into the ch or ch-sp of the open sp below, or into the dc of the filled sp below.

Working with Gauge

If you make an apple pie and I make an apple pie, and we use the same ingredients and the same recipe, will the two dishes be just alike?. . . Well, maybe. A lot depends on how we measure out the ingredients. You may be careful and precise, leveling each teaspoon and measuring cup. I may work more casually, adding ingredients with a slightly more generous hand. The difference in the way we measure, along with a number of other variables, will cause a difference in the finished product. They may be equally as good, but they will be different.

If you want to make a crocheted piece that will be exactly the size given in a set of instructions (this can be critical in making a garment and may be important to you, as well, when you are making an afghan or other decorative piece), you should know that the same yarn, worked into the same number of stitches, with the same size hook, can make pieces of varying sizes, depending on whether the crochet is worked with a tighter or looser tension.

In cooking, a carefully measured teaspoon is a standard measurement (though recipes may allow some room for individual preferences of "a bit more, a bit less.") In crochet, the amount of yarn measured into each stitch is very much a matter of individual style. One crocheter may stitch in a manner that is firm and precise; another may work with a looser, more relaxed technique. If the finished effect is pleasing, either style is perfectly correct. The problem comes when a difference in tension causes the finished work to be a different size from that intended by the instructions. The solution is in a note attached to almost every set of instructions, labeled **gauge.**

Gauge: 7 sts = 2″, 3 rows = 1″—for example—is not really the cryptic command it may seem, but a friendly note from the designer saying, "If you stitch, as I do, so that 7 sts measure 2″ and 3 rows measure 1″, this piece will finish up the size I've given you above, approximately 57″ x 66″." In order to match that finished size, you'll have to first find out if your stitches match those of the designer in size. (Don't worry; if they don't, there is a simple solution.)

To check the size of your stitches against the designer's, make a **gauge swatch**. Working with the yarn and hook you intend to use for the piece, stitch a sample block of the pattern to be used in the afghan at least 4″ square. (A swatch smaller than this is not an accurate test of your tension). Using a ruler and pins or a knitters' gauge measure, measure an inch or two inches (whatever measurement is given in the gauge note); count and compare the number of stitches or rows in your work and the designer's gauge.

If there is a difference between your work and the gauge measurement, you can try to alter your tension by working a bit more tightly or loosely, especially if your current tension is so extreme that the effect of the finished fabric is not what you want. However, if your stitches are generally even and the fabric is well-made, the best way to adjust for gauge is to change the size of the hook you are using. If you have too few stitches in your swatch, use a smaller hook; if you have too many stitches, try a larger hook. Remake the gauge swatch and measure again. When your stitches and rows per inch match those of the designer, following the instructions should result in a piece the same size as the original.

One final word about gauge: Your tension will vary with the hook and materials you are using, and with your mood. If you are tired or tense, your working tension may be different. It may change, too, as you become more familiar with the pattern and therefore more relaxed in the work. It's a good idea to check gauge several times during the course of any given project. Keep several sizes of hooks on hand so that you can adjust for variations in your personal style of working.

EXPLORING COLOR

Begin your adventures in crochet color by exploring your local yarn shop. Scan the shelves; flip through sample books. You'll find an abundance of color—clear, sunny primaries and delicate pastels; deep, rich jewel colors and muted earth tones.

With such riches to draw from, even a monochromatic color scheme—one based on a single, carefully chosen color—can be pleasing, especially when a highly textured stitch lends interest to the design. For examples of charming simplicity of color, see Popcorn Afghan (page 76) or Lace & Linens (page 102).

Another way to achieve interesting effects using only a single strand is to choose a variegated yarn. Study the effects of multicolored yarns, used singly and in combination, in Mossy Stones (page 66).

One of the simplest ways to manipulate two colors is to hold two strands of different colored yarn together as you work, producing a heathery effect. The colored stripes in Lace & Lavender (page 22) are made by holding white sportweight yarn and various shades of lavender pearl cotton together as you stitch.

For another easy way to play with color, work contrasting yarns into simple stripes, as in our Over the Rainbow afghan (page 47). The only special technique you'll need to know is **how to change color at the end of the row:** In the last stitch of the last row before the color change, use the new yarn color for the final yarn over and for the turning chain. By doing this, you will make the entire first stitch of the new row in the new color. Clip the loose end to six inches and weave it carefully into the work.

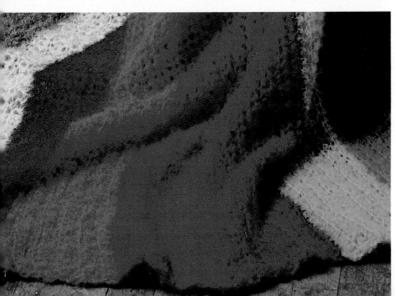

119

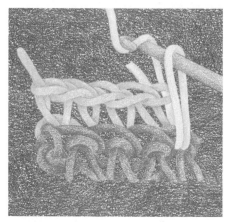

Joining with Slip Stitch

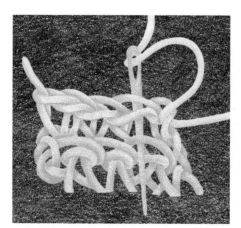

Joining with Whipstitch

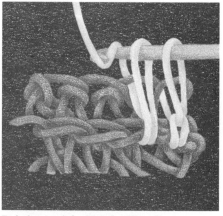

Joining with Single Crochet

Some designs require that you make blocks or strips of different colors and join them together (as in Log Cabin Afghan, page 84, or Peach Delight, page 30). Pieces can be joined with various stitches, including slip stitch, whipstitch, or single crochet. Joining stitches can be worked through two loops of each stitch to be joined or through the back loop or front loop only of each stitch. (Working through only one loop will result in a ridged effect.)

Or embellish your afghan with touches of embroidery. Cross-stitch designs can be worked from a color-coded chart, just as if you were working on evenweave fabric. The background in this instance, however, is crocheted afghan stitch, a specially worked stitch that forms a dense, firm fabric "gridded" with squares. See Sailing, Sailing (page 42) or Indian Blanket (page 62) for examples.

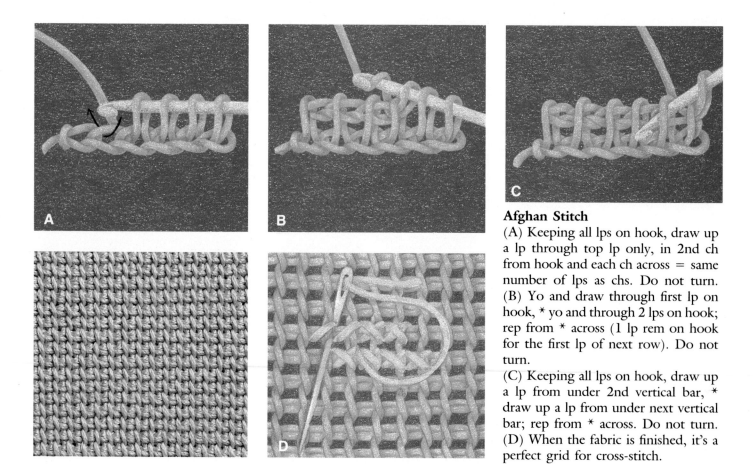

Afghan Stitch

(A) Keeping all lps on hook, draw up a lp through top lp only, in 2nd ch from hook and each ch across = same number of lps as chs. Do not turn.
(B) Yo and draw through first lp on hook, * yo and through 2 lps on hook; rep from * across (1 lp rem on hook for the first lp of next row). Do not turn.
(C) Keeping all lps on hook, draw up a lp from under 2nd vertical bar, * draw up a lp from under next vertical bar; rep from * across. Do not turn.
(D) When the fabric is finished, it's a perfect grid for cross-stitch.

Chain Stitch

Fly Stitch

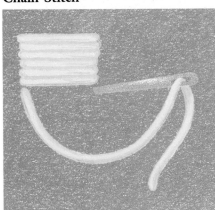

Satin Stitch

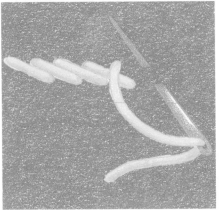

Stem Stitch

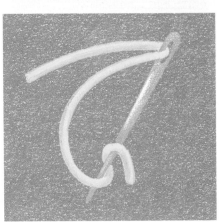

French Knot

Other types of embroidery, as well, can lend color to your afghans; see Folk Art Florals (page 79) or Pennsylvania Dutch (page 57). To achieve these effects, first crochet the background according to the instructions and add the embroidered design using the stitches shown above.

The most sophisticated way to work with color in your afghans is to work a pattern of various colors into the stitches as you go (see Flower Cart Afghan, page 24). Working in this way means that you will need to handle two or more yarns at the same time, while you follow directions for color changes. Directions for simple color changes may be expressed in words in the instructions; more complex color patterns may be shown in a color-coded stitch chart. To follow either type of direction, you will need to know how to change colors within the row and deal with floats, or yarn colors not in use at any given time.

To change to a new color within the row: Lay the end of the new-color yarn loosely on top of the row you are working, several stitches before the color change is to occur. Work over the new yarn end with your old color, covering the new color and securing the loose end in the work as you go. On the last stitch before the color change, make the final yarn over with the new color yarn; this means that the next stitch will be entirely in the new color. If you are finished with the old color, carry it along for a few stitches, covering it with the new yarn just as before, and clip the old yarn once it has been secured in the work.

On the other hand, if you will need the old color again, carry it along as a "float." You can continue to work over it with the new yarn, or, if for any reason the new yarn does not successfully cover the old color (if, for instance, you are working with several colors and cannot easily cover all the floats), let the floats drop behind the stitches on the wrong side of the piece, until you pick them up again. Make sure that the floats are not carried too loosely or so tightly that they pucker the work.

To work with a large number of colors wind the different colors of yarn on bobbins; twist the old color over the new at each color change to avoid holes in your work.

EXPLORING TEXTURE

The easiest way to incorporate interesting textures into your crochet is by relying on the texture of the yarn itself. Compare the smooth, resilient acrylic of Game Birds (page 72), to the feathery soft mohair used in Frosted with Pink (page 16), and the velvety chenille of Confection in Chenille (page 15) for a small sampling of the variety available.

By working these yarns into the stitch patterns that make up each afghan, you, as needleworker, build the fabric of each design, with its own special texture. The written instructions for each piece give you the guidance you need to achieve each new texture; but in order to follow those instructions, you must become familiar with certain more advanced ways of working. For example, working in one loop only—either front or back—of the stitch in the row below, rather than the usual two loops, gives a ridged effect. Working between stitches gives a raised effect. Making the loop stitch adds yet another textural detail. Use the diagrams shown on the following page to learn some of the techniques you'll need for various stitch patterns.

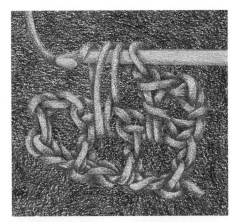

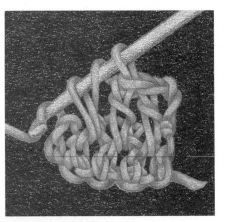

Working in Back Loop Only   **Working into a Chain Space**   **Working Between Stitches**

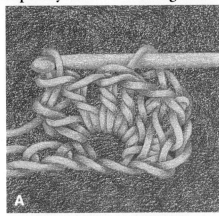

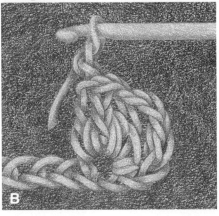

Working a Cluster of Stitches

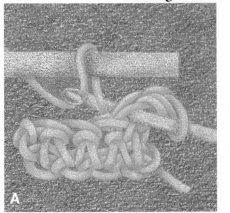

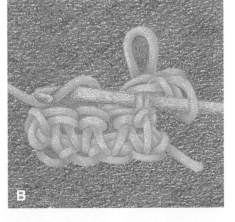

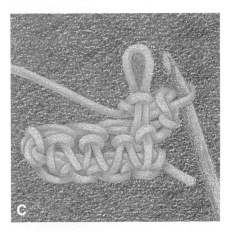

Loop stitch

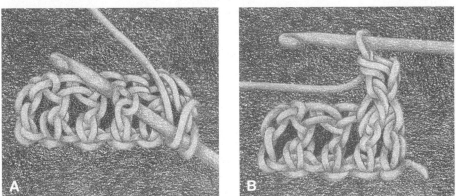

Working Around the Post

123

Single Crochet Edging

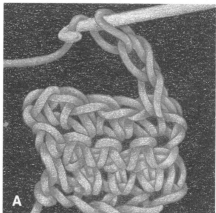

Picot Edging

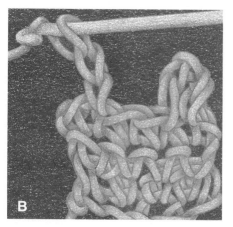

FINISHING THE PIECE

You may finish your afghan with any number of special edgings. Instructions for each afghan give the designer's choice. Among the edgings used are single crochet, reverse single crochet (single crochet worked left to right, instead of right to left), and picot.

If you wish, make a single or double knot fringe as a final accent to your afghan. Choose a dominant color (as in Blueberries 'n Cream, page 44) or harmonize colors used throughout the piece by making a multicolored fringe (as in Falling Leaves, page 70).

CARING FOR CROCHET

Store finished crochet as you would any fine textile; protect it from intense light and extremes of temperature and humidity. Don't wrap crocheted pieces in plastic bags (which do not allow air to circulate) or place crochet directly on bare wood surfaces. Instead, wrap pieces in cotton muslin or cotton pillowcases.

Be sure to save yarn labels for reference; they contain valuable information on cleaning and caring for your afghan.

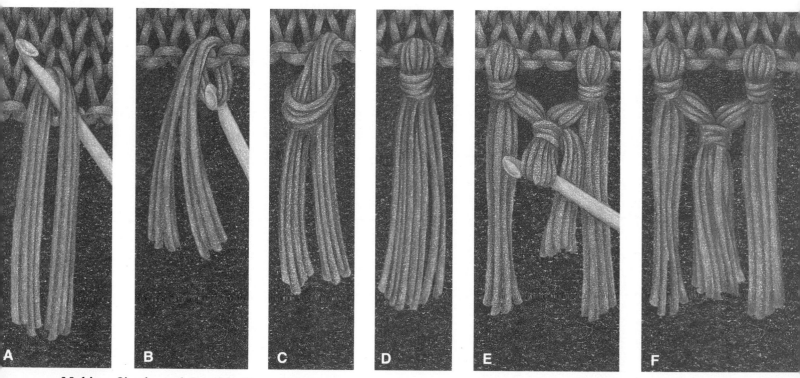

Making Single and Double Knot Fringe

YARN SOURCES

To obtain the yarns suggested for each project, check with your local needlework shop. For further information on sources, write the following customer service addresses.

Bernat Yarn & Craft Corporation
Depot and Mendon Streets
Uxbridge, MA 01569

Berroco, Inc.
Elmdale Road
Uxbridge, MA 01569

Brunswick Yarns
P.O. Box 276
Pickens, SC 29671

Caron International
Attention: Consumer Service
Avenue E and First Street
Rochelle, IL 61068

Classic Elite Yarns
12 Perkins Street
Lowell, MA 01854

Coats & Clark, Inc.
P.O. Box 1010
Dept. CS
Toccoa, GA 30577

Columbia-Minerva
McBess Industries
Box 1240
East Virginia Avenue
Bessemer City, NC 28016

DMC Corporation
107 Trumbull Street
Elizabeth, NJ 07206

Laines Anny Blatt USA, Inc.
24770 Crestview Court
Farmington Hills, MI 48331

Lily Craft Products
B. Blumenthal, Inc.
140 Kero Road
Carlstadt, NJ 07072

Lion Brand Yarn Company
34 W. 15th Street
New York, NY 10011

Mark Distributors, Inc.
5239-B Commerce Avenue
Moorpark, CA 93020

National Yarn Crafts
183 Madison Avenue
New York, NY 10016

Neveda Yarn Company, Inc.
(for Neveda and Scheepjeswol yarns)
199 Trade Zone Drive
Ronkonkoma, NY 11779

Patons Yarn
212 Middlesex Avenue
Chester, CT 06412

Phildar, USA
6110 Northbelt Parkway
Atlanta, GA 30071

Pingouin Yarn
P.O. Box 100, Highway 45
Jamestown, SC 29453

Reynolds Yarns
A Division of Johnson
    Creative Arts, Inc.
445 Main Street
West Townsend, MA 01474

Scheepjeswol yarns
(see Neveda Yarn Company, Inc.)

William Unger & Company, Inc.
P.O. Box 1621
Bridgeport, CT 06601

Contributors

PHOTOGRAPHERS
Tom Arma
    12-13
Jim Bathie
    73, 105
Billy Brown
    96-97, 98
Van Chaplin
    67
Colleen Duffley
    cover, 6-7, 8-9, 19, 22, 31, 34-35, 36, 37, 38, 43, left 48, 60-61, 62, 63, 71, 82, 86-87, 89, 90-91, 112, 113, 114, 120
Mary-Gray Hunter
    18, 24, 47, 79
Mac Jamieson
    25
Beth Maynor
    17, 32, 54, 69, 99, 107
John O'Hagan
    15, 20, 51, 65, 66, 77, 95
Gary Parker
    57, 58, 85, 100, 102-103
Melissa Springer Rogers
    10, 41, 44, 45, 48-49, 70, 83, 88, 92, 117

SPECIAL THANKS
Special thanks to the following companies, who furnished materials, afghans, and other design support for this book:

Bernat Yarn & Craft Corporation
Brunswick Yarns
Caron International
Classic Elite Yarns
Coats & Clark, Inc.
Columbia-Minerva
DMC Corporation
DuPont Company
Laines Anny Blatt USA, Inc.
Lion Brand Yarn Company
Mark Distributors, Inc.
Memory Hagler Knitting, Etc.
National Yarn Crafts
Neveda Yarn Company, Inc.
Patons Yarn
Phildar, USA
Pingouin Yarn
Reynolds Yarns
William Unger & Company, Inc.

To find out how you can order *Cooking Light* magazine, write to *Cooking Light* ®, P.O. Box C-549, Birmingham, AL 35283